Information Technology

Hwfa Jones

In association with the
Thames Valley Information Technology Unit

Consultant Editor: Joyce Stananought

Chambers Commerce Series

© Thames Valley Information Technology Unit 1989

Published by W & R Chambers Ltd Edinburgh, 1989

British Library Cataloguing in Publication Data
Jones, Hwfa
 Information Technology
 1. Office Procedures. Information
 systems
 1. Title
 651

ISBN 0-550-20713-9

Typeset by Bookworm Typesetting Ltd, Edinburgh

Printed in Great Britain by
Richard Clay Ltd, Bungay, Suffolk

Contents

Preface

This book describes the main features of the information revolution that is changing the world we live in. It is a straightforward guide to information technology which includes the most up-to-date developments and shows how they came about. Although primarily designed as a comprehensive reference text for students, it is also ideally suited to the reader who wishes to keep abreast of the changes which are all around us.

Each chapter covers the essentials of the subject area in clearly headed sections and is followed by a series of questions or assignments.

H.J.

Chapter 1

Introducing IT

Information technology (IT) is the major boom industry of the western nations and the countries of the Pacific. Fuelled by the development of the silicon chip a quarter century ago, it has grown explosively, and today consumer products of all types are controlled by chips.

1.1 Examples of IT

Here's just two of many examples of chip-controlled products.

- My friend used to take hopeless snapshots, as he could never get the aperture and focusing right. So I bought him one of those neat auto-everything cameras. He merely has to aim it, and the chips inside do everything else. Perfect pictures every time!
- Your telephone might contain chips allowing it to auto-dial certain numbers. This not only saves you the bother of looking up numbers and dialling, it cuts out misdialling.

The world of work is being rapidly transformed by IT and the silicon chip. In the office, all kinds of tasks – from writing to record keeping – are now being aided by the chips inside computers. In the factory, computer terminals and robots are becoming commonplace, and the whole production process – from design to storage and distribution – is coming under computer control.

The commercial development of IT is also having a significant military spin-off. Computerised battle control systems and deadly accurate chip-based weapons systems are just two of the applications.

All areas of life – the home, leisure, transport, communications, the office, and the factory – are being revolutionised by IT and the silicon chip. This book will cover, in an easily-understood way, all aspects of this information revolution, especially those that will help to prepare you for the world of work.

1.2   Is IT a Good Thing?

Some will say that my friend's camera takes away much of the skill and interest of photography. However, he rarely took any pictures with his old camera. Now, instead of being bothered with the technicalities of measuring light strengths and distances, he can concentrate on what's important, which is the composition of the picture.

I'm writing this book on a computer. I don't have to concern myself with things like numbering the sections, or altering the numbering if I rearrange the sections, or numbering the pages, or making sure that a heading is not left hanging at the foot of one page, with its text on the next. The computer does all that for me, leaving me free to concentrate on composing the material. Not only that, but I don't have to retype whole pages if I make a number of changes, and the manuscript that I send to the publisher will be free of crossings out and Tippex. I find that I can write twice as fast as before the days of computers, and the finished result is much better.

So is IT a good thing? I'm sure it is, as:

- I now earn more money
- I have more leisure time
- The boring parts of my job are done by my computer.

Besides this, there are other advantages. For example, my written material is stored on small computer disks instead of on reams and reams of paper. I can use my computer for many other tasks besides writing, and it occupies much less space than the several items of equipment (typewriter, accounting machine, etc.) that it replaces.

That's not to deny that the information revolution has caused problems. There have been many technological revolutions in human history. They have all resulted in changes in work and in lifestyles. New jobs have been created, but old jobs have disappeared. People have become better off, but they have had to go through years of uncertainty and change.

So the information revolution has brought great opportunities, especially at work, and at the same time a number of problems. I shall be examining its effects on work and on jobs in the final chapter. For you, the bottom line is: 'How will it affect me?' Well, that depends to a large extent on your attitude towards it. The opportunities are there – are you willing to grasp them?

1.3   What is IT?

Let's think about the steps I need to take to use the auto-dial features on my telephone.

- To begin with, I have to key in the number I wish the instrument to store. In other words, my phone has to *capture* the information.
- I also have to press the 'store' key to tell it to *store* this information.
- Later, when I wish to dial the number, I press a key marked 'memory' to *retrieve* the number.
- The phone then *processes* this stored information by converting it to a code of electrical pulses understood by the telephone exchange.
- It then *communicates* the information by sending the pulses down the phone line.

All IT devices work in this way. They capture, store, retrieve, process, and communicate information. This is often illustrated by the kind of diagram shown in Figure 1.1. The arrows in the figure represent the flow of information through these stages.

Fig. 1.1 *How an IT device works*

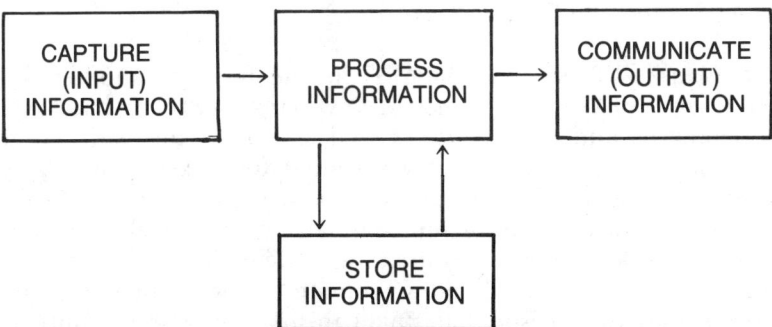

In the case of phone dialling, the information takes the form of numbers. We call this type of information *data*. However, information can take many forms. In the case of this book, the information takes the form of *text*. In the case of my friend's camera it takes the form of *image*, and in the case of any phone calls I make it takes the form of *voice*.

IT is concerned with the capture, storage, retrieval, processing, and communication of information in all these forms. Often, the same system can handle all of them. For example, today's phone network is not just used for voice: data can be sent over it from one computer to another, text sent from one teletext machine to another, and image sent from one fax machine to another.

Based on this, here's a simple definition of IT that covers everything from my friend's camera to my phone and my computer:

> Information technology is the use of technology to aid the capture, storage, retrieval, processing, and communication of information, whether in the form of data, text, image, or voice.

There's plenty of other more complicated definitions, but they all say essentially the same thing. Here's the one offered by the Northern Examination Association:

> Information technology is the study of information handling and its use in society by means of modern technology. This includes the acquisition, processing, storage and communication of information in any form by appropriate means. Within information technology there is an identifiable body of subject content, skills and activities. This common core is transferable, relevant to other curriculum areas and has wide application in society.

1.4   IT and the Silicon Chip

Of course, IT has been with us in one form or another for thousands of years. The ancient Egyptians used IT in the form of papyrus and quill pens, as well as simple calculating and measuring aids. The Chinese invented the abacus. But these developments hardly revolutionised society in the way that iron smelting did a couple of millenia ago, or the development of machinery a couple of centuries ago. The IT revolution only took off two or three decades ago with the development of the silicon chip. What is it that makes this device so important?

Computers were developed about half a century ago, but those first models were large, expensive, unreliable, and not very powerful. They were based upon glass valves, the kind of thing that was used in early radios and TVs. The significance of valves for computing is that they can be used as switches. Apply a current along one wire, and the valve is turned ON allowing a second current to flow along another wire. Switch off the first current, and the valve is turned OFF and the second current stops flowing.

That doesn't sound much like computing, until you realise that an ON valve can represent the digit 1 and an OFF valve can represent the digit 0. String thousands of these valves together, and you can have lots of 1s and 0s. And if that doesn't sound like it's much help, think back to the binary code that you met at school:

Zero is represented by 0 in binary

One is represented by 1

Two is represented by 10

Three is represented by 11

Four is represented by 100

Five is represented by 101

and so on.

So any number can represented by a string of 0s and 1s, or *binary digits* as they are often called. This means that numbers can be stored by sequences of ON and OFF valves. By organising some of these valves in special circuits called *logic gates*, numbers can also be added together and subtracted, and by an extension of this, multiplied and divided.

And that, in essence, was how the early computers worked. They had lots of valves used for storing numbers, and some valves arranged in special circuits for calculating. They also had input devices to capture the numbers in the first place, and output devices (i.e. special computer printers) to communicate the results.

Then, towards the end of the 1940s, the transistor was developed. This was a much smaller type of switch, based upon the special properties of silicon. Now, a single tiny wafer of this substance could store a 1 or 0, or be incorporated in a logic gate to perform calculations. Not only was the transistor smaller than a valve, it was cheaper to make and much more reliable, and it consumed much less electricity. This meant that:

- Computers could be made much smaller and more cheaply.
- They could contain many more switches and logic gates, and therefore handle more data and perform more calculations at greater speed.

After a number of years a way was found of putting two transistors on a sliver of silicon, and then four, and then eight. In fact, the number of transistors per chip has been doubling every 18 months ever since. This means that more and more power has been crammed into ever smaller and cheaper circuitry. It is this repeated doubling of power, continuing for a quarter of a century or more, that has caused the information revolution.

1.5   Information and Bits

The term 'binary digit' is normally shortened to *bit*. Some types of silicon chip are used to store bits – these are called memory chips. Other types of chip perform calculations on bits – these are called processing chips, or more commonly, *microprocessors*. Computers have both kinds inside their casing, the former to store data temporarily while the computer is working on it, the latter to carry out the calculations.

The earliest computers were used to handle numerical data, and they were applied to scientific and engineering calculations. Modern computers, of course, can handle information in all forms. But since chips and computers deal in numbers, how can they cope with text, image, and voice?

The answer is that this non-numerical information has to be converted to bits. For example, each letter of the alphabet is coded by the computer. When I press the letter 'A', a string of electrical pulses representing a sequence of 0s and 1s is sent to the memory chip where it switches a string of the tiny transistors to a corresponding sequence of ON and OFF states. The most common coding system is called *ASCII* (short for 'American Standard Code for Information Interchange'). In this, the letter 'A' is represented by the binary number 01000001 (i.e. OFF-ON-OFF-OFF-OFF-OFF-OFF-ON), the letter 'B' by 01000010, the letter 'C' by 01000011, and so on.

The image from a video camera can also be convered to this

kind of 'digital' form and handled by chips, as can sound from a microphone. That's why computers, like the telephone network, are able to handle all forms of information.

You may have noticed that those strings of bits I've listed above are eight digits long. Right from the earliest days of computing, valves and transistors were organised in groups of eight to store data. These groups of eight bits are called *bytes*, which is probably a shortened form of 'by eight'. In the case of data or text, each byte represents one letter or number.

1.6 IT and Laser Light

Besides the silicon chip, the development of *laser light* is intimately associated with the IT revolution. This differs from ordinary light in two ways:

- It has a single frequency, so one source of laser light can easily be picked out from others – very important when light is used to transmit information.
- It is projected as a very narrow, intense beam, and so is not dissipated much when it travels over a long distance.

So laser light makes an ideal medium for communicating digital information. It represents a binary 1 by a short pulse of laser light, and a binary 0 by the absence of a pulse. These pulses can be sent down an optic fibre in the case of a telecommunications system, or, in the case of a compact disc, they can be used to burn tiny pits in its surface. These pits similarly represent 1s and 0s, so storing the information in digital form. I shall be dealing with the use of laser light for communicating and storing information in Chapters 7 and 8.

1.7 Conclusion

If the binary code doesn't make much sense to you, don't worry. It isn't necessary to know anything about it in order to use computers and IT, any more than you need to understand the workings of the internal combustion engine to drive a car.

However, you should know what a bit is and what a byte is, as you will come across these terms again. I'll mention here too the word *kilobyte*, normally shortened to Kbyte or just K, meaning one thousand bytes (1024, to be exact), and the word *megabyte*, normally shorted to Mbyte, meaning one thousand Kbytes (1024K to be exact), i.e. a million bytes. Modern computers and other IT devices handle data in these sorts of quantities, and so you will meet these terms also from time to time.

You should also be aware of the need for modern IT equipment to handle data in digital form, i.e. as strings of 0s and 1s. In the past, most information-handling equipment worked with information in analogue (i.e. wave) form. The telephone is a good example, as this was originally developed to carry voice, transmitting it by electrical waves travelling along the phone wires.

To keep up with the IT revolution, phone networks are being digitised, so that in the future they will send data as streams of pulses, the presence of a pulse indicating a binary 1, the absence indicating a binary 0. In the case of phone wires, these will take the form of electrical pulses; however, much of the network is being replaced by the much powerful optic fibres, in which case laser light pulses will be used.

You will learn more about all this later in the book. You will also learn something of the plans to digitise other types of information handling equipment, including the radio and TV networks, so that all kinds of devices can be interconnected to form an integrated information-handling system. 'Integrated home systems', for example, are being developed to link together central heating, burglar alarms, telephone, cooker, TV, computer, etc. to provide an 'intelligent' environment in which to live.

The information revolution is only just beginning.

Questions

1 List four advantages of using a piece of modern IT equipment such as a computer or the auto-dial mechanism on a phone instead of old fashioned equipment such as a typewriter or a manual-dial phone.

2 A computer consists of four essential parts. What are they?

3 How is the letter D stored on a silicon chip if the ASCII code is used?

4 Many memory chips can store 8 Kbytes of data. How many bits is this?

5 How many pages of this book do you think could be stored in an 8 Kbyte memory chip?

6 Think of two advantages that will result from the digitisation of the phone network.

Chapter 2

Computers

As you learned in the last chapter, a computer consists of memory chips to store data, processing chips to process data, input devices to capture data, and output devices to communicate the results of the processing.

You learned too that many other items of IT equipment, such as my auto-dial phone, also consist of these devices. What, then, makes computers so different and so important? The answer is that computers are incredibly versatile. The auto-dial mechanism on my phone can only auto-dial, whereas my computer can do a very large number of things – including auto-dialling.

I use my computer not only to write books, but also to keep my diary, to handle my accounts, keep records such as names and telephone numbers (and to dial up those numbers automatically for me), and even to access over the telephone network my bank account in the home banking section of Prestel. Besides this, my son uses it to produce designs for CDT assignments at school, not to mention the computer games he plays on it.

In the world of work, the computer can be attached to many other devices, so increasing its versatility still further. To give just three out of many possibilities, it can be attached to:

- laser printers to produce magazine and brochures of the highest quality;
- videodisc players to provide powerful education and training sessions combining video and computer material;
- machine tools in the factory to automate manufacture.

Computers, in fact, lie at the heart of IT.

2.1 Why are Computers so Versatile?

Increasing digitisation of equipment is the reason why computers can be connected to so many devices. But this does not address the question of why computers are so versatile, able to do a large range of jobs, either by themselves or connected to other devices. The answer to this is that, unlike other equipment, the computer is not prewired to perform a fixed sequence of operations, but instead holds its instructions in the form of a stored program. And the crucial thing about a stored program is that it can be changed at any time, so altering what the computer does.

If I wish to use my computer to write books, I run a word processing program. If I use it to keep records, I run a record-keeping program. If I use it to access my bank account over the telephone line, I run a communications program. I have many dozens of different programs that I can use, hence the versatility of my computer. (However, if I had no programs at all, my computer would be completely useless, unable to do anything.)

2.2 Hardware and Software

The 'hard' bits of the computer – the casing, keyboard, circuitry, etc. – are called the *hardware*. Once you have bought a computer, you are stuck with the hardware until it breaks down completely (most unlikely) or you put it in a cupboard because it has become obsolete.

The programs that tell the computer what to do are different, for they can be replaced at any time. When you have finished with one, you simply run another. As well as this, you could, if you were a programmer, alter any of the programs so that they behave differently. Because they are not immutably fixed in cast-iron casings, programs are called *software*.

A computer system consists of both hardware and software. I shall deal with the hardware in this chapter, and introduce software in the next.

In many ways a computer handles a program just like it handles ordinary data or text. To run a program, it captures it (i.e. loads it) via the same devices that it uses to input data. One input device is the keyboard, but because programs are so long it is not practical to type them in every time you wish to use them. Instead, they are normally stored in *files* on computer disks (see later), and read into the computer via the *disk drive*.

Once in the computer, the program is stored alongside any data in the memory, and it makes use of the computer's processing power to interpret and perform the instructions that it contains.

So when I began work for the first time on this book earlier today, I started by running my word processing program, and then I began typing in the text. Periodically I save the text on disk, in a file that is quite separate from the word processing program file. Tomorrow, when I resume work, I will load in first the word processing software, and then the file of text.

You do not, of course, need to be able to write or understand computer programs in order to benefit from computers. You merely have to be able to use the programs, and one of the purposes of this book is to tell you how.

2.3   Types of Computer

There are many different kinds of computer, which is a testimony to the rapid and healthy growth of the IT industry. What is unhealthy is the fact that different types of computer are normally incompatible, meaning that you can't run software written for one on another, at least not without at least some conversion work. (There are exceptions to this, and I will deal with some of them below.) This section introduces some of the main types of computer.

Computers are normally split into three broad classes: *mainframe computers*, *minicomputers*, and *microcomputers*.

a) Mainframe computers
So called because of the big metal frame that holds the processing unit, mainframes are the largest type of computer, occupying a whole room and able to support many dozens of different programs and users at the same time.

Each user will have a console or *VDU* (short for 'visual display unit') consisting of a keyboard for input and a screen for output. By a technique known as *multiprogramming*, the computer will switch its processing from one user to the next, the speed of switching being so fast that to the individual user it seems as if he or she is the only one on the system.

Mainframe computers cost upwards of £100 000, they require a number of trained operators to carry out essential system tasks, and are used in only the largest organisations. They are able to handle very large data processing tasks, such as the payroll for many thousands of employees, or the seat reservations system of an airline.

b) Minicomputers

You can think of a minicomputer as a cut-down version of a mainframe. It can handle the work of a number of users simultaneously, though not as many as can a mainframe. It can also handle fairly large jobs. Minicomputers are much smaller than mainframes, and the smallest can sit on a desk.

c) Microcomputers

Microcomputers are intended for use by only one person at a time. In recent years this has changed somewhat, and some micros will allow *multiuser* working, though few are actually ever used like this.

Microcomputers fall into two broad camps, namely *personal computers* used primarily for work and business purposes, and *home computers* used primarily for home and recreational purposes.

By far the most important type of computer is the personal computer. Personal computers are becoming increasingly powerful, they are supported by a huge range of software, and most people today will use one for at least some of their work. You will probably use them at your college, so in this book I shall concentrate mainly on this type of computer.

2.4 Personal Computers

The main sort of personal computer is the IBM Personal Computer (including compatible machines, or 'clones', from other manufacturers). These are normally called PCs, short for 'personal computer'. At present, the most popular version of this is the AT, short for 'Advanced Technology', and often referred to as the PC/AT. Actually this is not very advanced by today's standards, but it is perfectly adequate for almost all office tasks. There are now over ten million PCs and ATs world-wide. Despite the many brand names and models of this type of computer, they are all compatible, i.e. able to run the same software.

Figure 2.1 shows the personal computer I am using to write this book. It is an AT-compatible, running all the software that the IBM PC/AT and other clones will run, although it is a portable 'laptop' machine that looks very different to the usual PC.

The compatibility that exists between the various models of the PC is a tremendous blessing, and one reason for the widespread adoption of IT in business. Although IBM was not the first to

Fig. 2.1   *The Toshiba 3100 laptop computer*

bring out microcomputers when it launched the PC back in 1981, it made them respectable amongst business people. So businesses started to buy them, and, encouraged by this, software houses started to write numbers of excellent programs for them. This encouraged yet more people to buy the computers, which in turn made a larger market which more software houses entered. A benign circle set in, as more buyers encouraged more software, and more software encouraged more people to buy.

IBM had made its machine 'open architecture', meaning that it was easy to copy, and other manufacturers jumped on the bandwagon, producing their own compatible versions of the PC. This competition forced down the price, which encouraged yet more people to buy. Today, this type of machine is very cheap, it is supported by, an unrivalled range of software, and it is the standard choice for business.

In 1987 IBM discontinued production of PCs and ATs, and brought out in their place its PS/2 range of machines (short for Personal System/2). These are able to run standard PC software, but they are capable of running more advanced programs as well.

They also have superior screen displays, which is an advantage for some software. A further advantage for users with IBM main-frames is that they can easily be connected to these to act as terminals or to access data stored on them. How successful the PS/2 range will prove only time will tell.

While IBM has been developing its product range, the manu-facturers of AT-clones have not been idle, and more powerful versions of these machines are becoming available (see below).

The other important type of personal computer is the Apple Macintosh. This is not compatible with the IBM PC/AT, but it is technically more advanced. Although it does not enjoy the same massive software support as the PC, there is a good range of business software for it, much of it of a very high standard.

The Apple Mac became a significant force in the business community as a result of its pioneering work in desktop pub-lishing. When low-cost laser printers appeared in the mid 1980s, the Apple Corporation realised that its machine, with its superior graphics capabilities, was well placed to take advantage of their high print quality. Desktop publishing (DTP) software was devel-oped to enable users of their computer to produce publications of a quality rivalling that of commercial typesetters, and the rest is history.

Even today, after great improvements in the hardware of IBM machines and compatibles, and the arrival on the PC scene of DTP software at least as good as that available for the Mac, the latter still remains the prime choice for DTP applications. It has to be said, however, that Apple and the Macintosh are tiny compared to the total size of the PC market, and the continuing development of PCs and PS/2s make it unlikely that the Mac will ever be a serious threat to those machines.

2.5 Computer Hardware

Figure 2.2 shows a schematic diagram of the parts of a computer system, from input through to output devices. I'll be explaining each of the devices shown in that figure in this part of the chapter.

First, though, here are a couple of terms you should know. The microprocessor chip (or chips) responsible for the processing is referred to as the *CPU*, short for 'central processing unit'. This is a hangover from the days when computers were all very large, having their various devices encased in separate units. For reasons that I'll explain below, the memory chips are referred to as *RAM*, short for 'random access memory'. 'Storage', in contrast to memory, refers to the long-term retention of data and software on disks.

Fig. 2.2   *Schematic of a computer system*

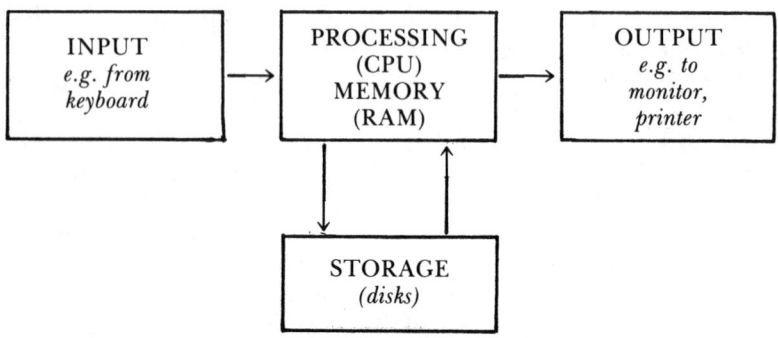

If all this seems a little strange at the moment, don't worry. You will have plenty of opportunity to become familiar with computers on this course, beginning with the assignment at the end of the chapter.

2.6   The CPU

The purpose of the microprocessor (CPU) chips is to execute whatever instructions are contained in the program currently running in the computer, so carrying out the processing required on the data or text that the user is working on. The CPU is therefore central to the computer's operations, and one of the main differences between the different types of computer is the different processing chips that they use. Here's a brief résumé of what these differences are.

First, chips for home computers are normally 8-bit. This means that they handle data 8 bits at a time. On personal computers, in contrast, most chips are either 16-bit or 32-bit. This not only means that they handle data at twice or four times the speed, it also means that they can support more memory and therefore cope with larger and more complex programs. 8-bit microprocessors can only access up to 64 K of memory, whereas 16- or 32-bit chips can normally access several Mbytes.

(One exception to this is the IBM PC/AT, which is limited to 640 K of memory. This is quite enough, though, for most office applications. It is not, enough, however, for complex graphics tasks, and it is certainly not enough if you want to *multi-task*, i.e. run several applications at the same time – see Chapter 3.)

Second, within these classifications there are a number of different types of chips. Amongst the 8-bit variety, the Z80 chip (made by Zilog) has been used since the mid-70s in business microcomputers, and it is supported by a good range of business software. The Amstrad PCW word processor has a Z80 chip, as does the Commodore 64. The BBC Micro, in contrast, has an 8-bit 6502 chip made by Mostek.

So far as personal computers are concerned, the most widely used chip is Intel's 8086 range used on IBM PC/ATs and compatibles, and the PS/2 range. PCs and PC-compatibles use the older 8086 chip, whereas ATs and the new PS/2s use the 80286 that appeared in 1984. The latter has many more transistors than the older chip, providing more functions and a higher processing speed.

More recently the much more powerful 32-bit 80386 chip has appeared. This not only offers more functionality and greater speed, it does not suffer the memory limitations of its older brethren. A large number of IBM-compatibles now use this chip. At the time of writing, Intel is about to launch its latest 80486 chip, and this should be very powerful indeed.

The main rival to the 80386 chip is the 32-bit 68000 series of chips from Motorola. These are used in the Apple Macintosh as well as in the newer 'hi-tech' machines such as the Atari ST and Commodore Amiga.

There are other important developments in the sidelines which are sure to have a major impact on computers in the future. One is the development of the transputer, i.e. 'transistor computer'. This is an entire computer – microprocessor and memory – on one chip. The significance of this is that transputers can be wired up in parallel so that they can all work on a job at the same time. This is called *parallel processing*, and mirrors the way in which the human brain behaves. It is anticipated that this type of processing will result in computers of very considerable power within a few years.

2.7 RAM

RAM is short for 'random access memory', and contrasts with the alternative 'sequential access'. To appreciate the difference, think about a music recording. This can be stored on either disc or cassette tape. In the former case, the stylus of the record player can be moved instantly to any point on the disc's surface to play a track – that's random access. In the latter case, however, you have to fast-wind the tape for a while until you reach the section you want – that's sequential access.

Memory chips are random access, so that data can be accessed from any location in them virtually instantaneously. Because of this, they are called *RAM* chips. They are used for the temporary storage of programs and data that are currently being used by the CPU. I say 'temporary' because RAM is *volatile*, meaning that anything stored in it is lost immediately the computer's power is turned off.

Memory is usually measured in Kbytes. Most modern personal computers can access up to 16 Mbytes of RAM, though few have more than 1 Mbyte installed. As I've said above, the IBM PC/AT is limited to 640 K of RAM.

2.8 Disk Drives

Because RAM is volatile and can only be used for temporary storage, a computer needs some form of non-volatile long-term storage device. At present, the main such storage device is the magnetic disk.

Like an audio cassette, information is recorded and read off one of these disks by a read/write head. However, unlike magnetic tape, this head can move to any spot on the surface of the disk very rapidly, and so it can access (i.e. store or retrieve) information at high speeds. So like memory chips, it is 'random access'. (The cassette tape storage system used on home computers is much too slow and unreliable for business use.)

Why are memory chips necessary – why not use disks for temporary and long-term storage? One answer is that, although they access information fast, disks are much slower than RAM chips, which would lead to painfully slow processing times.

As with everything else connected with computers, magnetic disks are digital devices. A magnetised spot on its surface represents a binary 1, and a demagnetised spot a 0. These 0s and 1s are laid down in circular tracks marked out magnetically on the disk's surface. As the disk rotates, an arm moves the read/write head to the required track, and 'reads' (i.e. retrieves) data from or 'writes' (i.e. stores) data to the spots on the track as they pass below it.

Most disk drives have two read/write heads, one to access data on the top of the disk, the second to access the other side. Both sides are treated by the computer as a single continuous surface.

a) Hard disks
Most personal computers have *hard disks* inside their casing. Even the portable computer I am using to write this book has a 20 Mbyte hard disk inside, though 40 Mbyte disks are more popular today. Most people can store all their software and all their current data and text files on a disk with this capacity.

Hard disks are rigid and quite heavy, and as a result they take several seconds to come up to speed. So they are kept constantly spinning (while the computer is turned on), even when data is not being accessed. The speed of rotation is a high 3600 revolutions per minute, which means that:

● Data is accessed at a very fast rate.
● The movement of the air molecules at the disk's surface lifts the read/write head just enough to prevent it touching the surface. This allows the head to access the data, but it does not cause any wear on the disk.

The disk and the head are enclosed in a sealed casing to prevent dust from getting onto the disk and interfering with the data access.

b) Floppy disks
Floppy disks are so called because they are light and flexible. Unlike hard disks, they are not sealed permanently inside the computer's casing, so they need to be stored in clean sleeves and containers. Also, you should not touch the exposed surface. The modern 3.5 inch variety is more secure, being encased in a protective plastic shell.

Also, the disk only spins when the data is being accessed, and the read/write head actually makes contact with the surface, causing slight wear. (This wear is of no consequence in normal use.)

If a computer has a hard disk, floppy disks are generally only used to transfer software or data between machines, and to store backups (copies) of data in case some mishap strikes the hard disk.

Floppy disks are not normally used apart from this, as compared to a hard disk they are:

● about ten times as slow, so that they take a (relatively) long time to access data;

● they can only hold a limited amount of data.

This means that if you want to run a large piece of software, you will have to retrieve it from several floppy disks, each of which takes several seconds to load. Furthermore, since not all parts of the software can be held in memory at the same time, you will have to keep inserting disks when you move from one function to another. This is very time-consuming and tedious compared to the ease and swiftness with which the same software runs from a hard disk.

The older 5.25 inch floppy disks can store only 360 K of data, though high-density versions are now available which can store 1.2 Mbytes. (These figures are for PC/ATs; other computers give slightly different capacities.) Note that low-density drives cannot access high-density disks, though high-density drives can access either.

In the case of the newer 3.5 inch disks, the low-density version stores 720 K, the high-density version around 1.4 Mbyte.

Note that all disks have to be formatted before they can be used. These means marking out on their surface the pattern of magnetic sectors required by the particular type of computer on which they are used. The system software supplied with computers (see next chapter) allows you to do this.

2.9   Input Devices

The keyboard is, of course, the main computer input device. As I've already explained, it works by converting key presses to electrical pulses in binary digital form. Computer keyboards follow the standard 'QWERTY' pattern of ordinary typewriter keyboards, with the addition of some further keys to perform special operations.

Some of the additional keys provided on most computers, including the PC, are listed below.

● Function keys, normally ten in number and marked F1 to F10, whose use varies according to the software package being run. For many pieces of software, F1 is the 'help' key, and pressing it displays a screen or more of explanatory material telling you about your current task. This saves you having to refer to the manual.
● The CTRL and ALT keys, short for Control and Alternative. These are always used in conjunction with other keys to perform special operations. Their function depends upon the

software being used. With the WordStar word processing software, for example, CTRL and T, pressed at the same time, deletes the word at the cursor position on the screen, and CTRL and Y deletes the line at this position. (To carry out these operations, you hold down the CTRL key, tap the keyboard key, then release CTRL.)

- The backspace key, which deletes the character to the immediate left of the cursor on the screen.
- The four 'arrow' keys, which move the cursor one character position in the direction of the arrow (up, down, left, or right).
- The ESC key, which is often programmed to allow you to escape from your current option or task.

The other commonly-used computer input device is the *mouse*, so called because it is about the same size and shape as a mouse (well, more like a fat hamster, actually), with a thin cable like a tail connecting it to the computer. As you push the mouse over the surface of your desk, the movements of the ball in its base are detected by some internal electronics and converted to electrical pulses. At the computer, these are converted to corresponding movements of the cursor across the screen.

At the front of the mouse are buttons which you press to select options displayed on the screen. The Apple Macintosh mouse has one button, most other types have either two or three.

I use the mouse a great deal with my word processing (writing) software, as it enables me to move rapidly around the screen when I want to alter my text. Also, it simplifies the job of picking options from the menus displayed across the top of the screen. I could, however, use the special keyboard keys instead, though these would be somewhat slower. The mouse really comes into its own if you are running a graphics program which involves you in a task like drawing on the screen. This task is almost impossible to do with the keyboard, but very easy with the mouse.

A number of other input devices can be connected to the computer. These include:

a) An optical character reader (OCR)
This device scans text which has been typed or printed on paper, converting the characters into the binary code that the computer understands. It provides a means of inputting pages of typed or printed material without having to re-key them. However, an OCR may not convert every character on the page correctly, and some corrections will have to be typed in to provide a perfect copy.

b) A scanner

This device works rather like a video camera connected to a computer, its function being to input photographs or other kinds of picture or drawing. The scanning mechanism is not a normal video camera but a row of charged-coupled devices (CCDs). Each CCD receives light from the image, and, provided the light is strong enough, generates an electrical charge.

You can think of the image as being broken up into many tiny areas. The bright areas of the image are represented by charged cells, and dark areas by uncharged cells. These charges create electrical pulses which are fed into the computer, a pulse representing a charged cell (a binary 1), the absence of a pulse representing an uncharged cell (a binary 0). At the computer, they are converted by the scanning software into the image.

The resolution (clarity) of the image produced by the typical scanner is 300 dots per inch (dpi), which means that it splits each square inch of the image up into a matrix of 300 by 300 tiny areas. This is better than the resolution of most computer screens, and the same as the resolution of most laser printers (see later in this chapter).

c) A microphone (for speech input)

A microphone with some additional electronics can be used to convert the spoken word to a digital signal for computer input. This does not mean, however, that you can throw away the keyboard and simply talk to the computer, for without some very sophisticated software the computer will not recognise the words that you speak. Even then, at the present state of the art, you have to speak fairly slowly.

Speech recognition systems face a number of problems. The first is that the English language is not phonetically precise. One simple example is the word 'to' – which sounds exactly the same as the word 'too' and the word 'two'. To decide which one you mean the computer has to examine the context of the words – just as we do when we are listening to someone talking.

The second problem is the wide variations between the speech patterns of one individual and another. To cope with this, the system has to be 'trained' to recognise your particular speech patterns. One way to do this is to read a set passage containing the words (or parts of words) stored in the computer's vocabulary on disk, so that it is able to match the spoken word with what's stored. It can then construct 'templates' for your particular speech patterns, which it can use in all subsequent dictation sessions.

The need to put words into context in order to recognise them requires an enormous amount of computing power, and a major drawback of speech recognition systems in the past has been the fact that they have been too slow to be of much use, or else they were limited to a vocabulary of just a few hundred words. Recent increases in computer power have greatly speeded things up, and now speech recognition systems are available – at a price – on personal computers.

No doubt as technology progresses, these systems will become more powerful and more popular, replacing the keyboard for many tasks.

2.10 Output Devices – Monitors

The main computer output devices are monitors (i.e. screens) and printers. Modems, needed to send the computer output down the telephone line to other computers, are dealt with in Chapter 6. I'll cover monitors in this section, printers in the next.

The resolution of the picture on the monitor screen is determined by the number of *pixels*, or 'picture elements' that it contains. High-resolution monitors have resolutions of 2000 by 2000 pixels, though few present-day computers are able to provide images which take advantage of that degree of clarity. The IBM PC, for example, with a colour graphics adaptor, can only output images with a resolution of 640 pixels horizontally by 200 vertically.

Desktop computers and terminals use cathode ray tubes, similar to those used on TVs. Portable computers use flat screens of various types. These various types of monitor are described below.

a) Cathode ray tubes (CRTs)
These consist of one or more 'guns' at the back of the tube which fire streams of electrons at a special chemical coating on the surface of the screen. These electron streams repeatedly scan the screen from top to bottom, dot by dot and line by line, each scan taking only a fraction of a second.

In the case of colour screens, there are three guns, one for each of the colours red, green and blue. These cause each dot on the screen to generate red, green, or blue light, the various combinations of these giving the full colour spectrum.

Monochrome monitors, in contrast, have only one gun, and they display text and graphics as either green on a black background, orange on a black background, or white on a black background. (These foreground and background colours can be reversed by software.) They give a much sharper picture than colour monitors, and are well suited for word processing and similar applications which do not require colour.

CRTs give a bright picture, but they are bulky and consume a relatively large amount of power.

b) Flat screens

Portable computers need screens which are light, occupy little space, and, in the case of battery-powered models, don't consume much power. The various types of flat screen meet this need, but, unlike CRTs, the image may not be very bright, and few flat screen monitors give colour displays.

Liquid crystal display (LCD) screens consume the least power, so they are used on battery-powered computers. The technology is similar to that used on digital watches. These screens do not emit any light themselves but are dependent on reflected light to be legible. The result is not always very successful, though the latest type of 'supertwist' display is quite good.

In an LCD screen, the image is formed by so-called liquid crystals. These are long rod-like molecules which, though solid, can flow like a liquid. Each pixel on the screen consists of a tiny electrode positioned below several of these molecules. As the output from the computer scans the screen a row at a time, it activates each of these pixels in turn, switching it on or off. When a pixel is 'on', the crystals twist in such a way that they block out the light, but when it is 'off' they let the light through.

Other types of flat screens are also available. One is the gas plasma display used on the Toshiba 3100 shown in Figure 2.1. These are light-emitting displays, and they give a very clear, legible output, typically orange on a brown background. However, because they emit light, these screens consume almost as much power as a CRT, and so are only suitable for mains-operated portable computers.

2.11   Output Devices – Printers

Computer printers provide a *hard copy* of computer output. Some printers have a print mechanism that is similar to that on a (modern) typewriter, and they are able to print only characters (letters, numbers, and a few special characters), not graphics. Others can also print graphics (image), e.g. drawings or charts.

Besides this difference, printers vary in their capabilities for enhancing text with emboldening and other effects.

Most printers are designed to receive data 'in parallel' from the computer, 8 bits at a time. These have to be connected to the parallel port (socket) on the computer. This is also called the *Centronics* port, and on PC/ATs it is labelled LPT1 (short for Line Printer 1).

Some printers, however, receive data 'in serial' from the computer, i.e. one bit at a time. These have to be connected to the serial port on the computer. This is also called the RS-232 port, and is sometimes labelled COM1 (short for Communications 1).

Printers also differ in a number of other ways.

● There are character printers (which print one character at a time), line printers (which print a line at a time), and page printers (which print a page at a time).
● A variety of printing technologies are possible, the main ones being dot matrix, daisy wheel, and laser.
● There are a variety of standards for *control codes*, which are commands sent from the computer to the printer to turn on effects such as underlining and emboldening.

With all these variations, it might seem surprising that anyone can ever get a printer to work with a computer. However, most software packages cope admirably with these differences by providing a range of *printer drivers*, i.e. programs which adapt the output from the software to match the requirements of the printer. All you have to do is select your printer's name from the list that is presented to you when you first use the software.

The main types of printer are described below. These are dot matrix and daisy wheel printers (both character printers), and laser printers (which are page printers). The main differences between them so far as the user is concerned are:

● their quality of output;
● whether they are able to print graphics;
● their print speed;
● their purchase price.

The print cost per page is generally around 2p per sheet, though it can be about half this in the case of dot matrix printers with reusable ribbons.

a) Dot matrix printers
These popular printers are inexpensive, fast, and able to print

graphics as well as text. The print mechanism consists of a matrix of tiny needles. By hitting selected needles so that they stand out from the rest, the printer is able to create the shape of a letter or other character, which it then prints on the paper by means of an inked ribbon. The print speed is typically 100 characters per second (cps) or more, and these printers are able to produce double size or very small characters as well as emboldening, italics, and other effects.

However, the print quality is not all that high, since the characters are not perfectly formed but consist of a pattern of dots. The resolution of most dot matrix printers is around 100 to 150 dots per inch, which is about half of what's necessary for a good quality result. To overcome this defect, many printers of this type offer a near-letter quality (NLQ) mode. When switched to this mode, the print head prints each line twice, the second pass slightly offset from the first, which has the effect of filling in the gaps between the holes and making the characters more perfectly formed. Naturally they print much more slowly in this mode, rather less than half their normal speed.

One of the original and most popular of the dot matrix printers for personal computers was the Epson FX-80. This has set a standard for control codes (for emboldening, graphics, etc.) which many other manufacturers of dot matrix printers have followed. Almost all software supports this standard, and today you can buy an Epson-compatible for as little as £150.

b) Daisy wheel printers

The print head used on this type of printer is a *daisy wheel*, a 3 inch diameter circular device which resembles a daisy flower. The print characters are embossed on the tip of each 'petal'. When printing, the wheel rotates to bring the required character uppermost, and a hammer strikes it against the ribbon to produce the printed impression on the paper. The print quality is very high, since the characters are perfectly formed.

The cheaper daisy wheel printers cost about the same as low-cost dot matrix printers, but they are much slower, generally printing at 13 to 15 characters per second.

c) Laser printers

Laser-beam printers, commonly called laser printers, are page printers, meaning that, rather like photocopiers, they print an entire page at a time. In fact, they resemble photocopiers in size and appearance, and they employ a similar technology. They are very fast, typical speeds for the desktop models being around eight pages per minute, and they are virtually silent in operation. The resolution of current models is 300 dots per inch, which is fine for office work and for publications which do not demand the extremely high quality associated with traditional typesetting.

These printers offer the versatility of the dot matrix – being able to produce text and graphics – with the quality of the daisy wheel, while being faster and quieter than either. They are more expensive, but prices of the cheapest models are now below £1000 and they are becoming increasingly popular. For desktop publishing, these printers are the only realistic choice.

2.12 Networked Computers

In many offices and colleges, computers are networked. This means that they are connected together by cable, able to communicate with each other and with items of equipment such as printers which may also be linked to the network. Files of software and data can then be passed from one machine to another; so can *electronic mail*, i.e. memos and other messages that are typed on the screen but not printed. (Electronic mail is sometimes called *email* for short.)

The advantages of having networked rather than stand-alone (i.e. unconnected) machines are as follows.

- Resources, such as hard disks and printers, can be shared, so cutting down on hardware costs.
- Files of data can be shared, so allowing all users to retrieve the same data and to keep the files up to date.
- Incompatible hardware, such as PCs and Apple Macs, can be linked via a network and files passed between them. This does not mean that Macs can use PC software or vice versa, but it does mean that files of data can be used by both.
- Data is less likely to be accidentally erased and lost, as formal procedures for carrying out tasks like making backups will be instituted. These backups will normally be made by the network manager.

In a network there will be a 'host' computer. This is the *file server*, so called because it holds, on its hard disk, the files used by the other computers on the network. (The file server may be able to act also as an ordinary networked computer, though the person using it may find that some operations are slowed down as part of its processing power is being tied up with looking after the network.) The other computers connected to the network may be called *stations* or *workstations*.

So far as personal computers are concerned, the most common type of network is the *local area network*, or LAN. In this, the various computers and other equipment are linked together by a single long coaxial cable laid around the site (see Figure 2.3). Besides this cabling, each computer must have a special piece of network circuitry on a small circuit-board or card installed inside its casing.

Fig. 2.3   *A local area network*

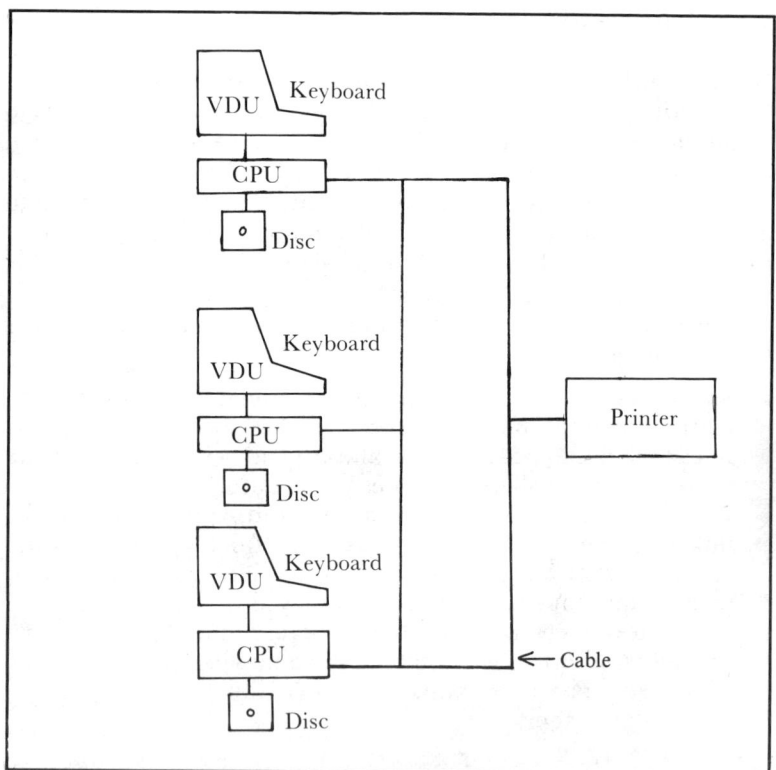

Messages (such as files of data) are sent round the network in small chunks or *packets,* each of which includes the 'address' of the receiving machine. A packet is 512 bytes in length. Each station constantly monitors the section of the cable to which it is connected, and captures from it any packets with its address.

A major problem with networks is ensuring that messages from one station do not interfere with those from another, resulting in both messages getting scrambled and lost. There are a number of possible solutions to this problem, resulting in different types of network system.

One of the most popular types of local area network is called *Ethernet*. In this, a station wishing to send information checks if there are any messages (packets) travelling round the cable. If there are not, it sends its message. If two stations, by chance, do this simultaneously, their messages interfere with each other and are lost. However, the fact that this has happened is signalled back to the two stations, and they each then wait a short random length of time and try again. As with most things in the computer world, all this takes place very rapidly, and the user is hardly aware of any delays.

Assignment 1

This assignment is in two parts. For the first part you have to do some research, and the second part requires you to practise using painting or drawing software on a computer. You will find it helpful to do the second part in conjunction with your reading of Chapter 3, which deals with software. Note that all personal computers (and home computers) are supported by painting and drawing software, and whether your college has BBC micros, PCs, or Macs, there is sure to be some software of this type available on them.

First, you should find out, from computer magazines or shops, the prices of the various components that make up a personal computer system. You can choose any type or brand, including Amstrad, Apple, Atari, or Acorn. Your prices should include the system box containing the CPU, RAM, and other electronics, as well as the monitor, the keyboard (if this is separate from the system box), the disk drives, and any suitable printer.

Next, using a computer with painting or drawing software, draw a diagram of these various components linked together in a system. Use the 'text' features of the software to label each component with its name and its price. Make sure that your diagram is headed with the brand name of the system and has your name at the foot, then print it out using a suitable printer and hand it in to your tutor.

Questions

1 Joe has a small decorating business, and he wishes to buy a computer system in order to run his accounts, produce estimates, invoice his customers, and write letters. What system would you advise him to buy? Give reasons for your choice.
2 Give three reasons for the spread of computing in business.
3 What are the differences between home computers and personal computers used in business?
4 Many people find the mouse a very useful input device. Why is this?
5 Although laser printers are relatively expensive, they are becoming very popular in the office. Give four reasons for this.

Chapter 3

Computer Software

Software is an essential part of a computer system. It is the programs of instructions that tell the computer what tasks to perform. With it, the computer can replace:

- the typewriter for writing jobs;
- the filing cabinet for record-keeping jobs;
- the calculator for calculating jobs;
- the drawing board for design jobs;
- the accounting machine for accounting jobs.

Besides making the computer so versatile, the software also makes the computer much better at these jobs than those machines ever were.

When you use a computer, there will be several pieces of software running in it at the same time.

- First, there will be *system software*, which tells the computer how to do its basic jobs like accessing disks, formatting disks, and controlling the screen display.
- Then there may be *environment software* which provides the user (i.e. you and me) with an easy-to-use way of getting the computer to run our word processing and other programs, to copy disks, and so on.
- Finally, there is the *application software* – word processing, record keeping, drawing, communications, games, and other programs – which enables us to apply the computer to writing and other tasks.

This chapter introduces you to these three kinds of software. Details on particular types of application software are covered in later chapters. First, though, a few words about how software is written.

3.1   Programming Languages

As I've said, computers deal in binary code, the language of 0s and 1s. The instructions that tell the computer what to do must be written in binary form, and in the earliest days of computing this was the 'language' that programmers had to use for their programs. It is called *machine code*.

Because machine code is intended for machines and not people, programmers found it very time-consuming and laborious to work with. So an easier programming language called *assembly language* was developed. In this, a single instruction replaces several machine code instructions, so speeding up the program-writing task. As well as this, assembly language instructions do not involve 0s and 1s, but use mnemonics instead – abbreviated words that represent the tasks to be performed and which can be easily remembered.

So assembly language programs were much easier to write. Of course, in order to be used by the computer, they had to be translated to the longer machine code instructions that the machine understands. The computer itself carries out this translation job. Every type of processor has its own assembling language and translation software, so assembly language programs written for the BBC micro (for example) will not work on the PC and vice versa.

Because machine code is the language of machines rather than people, and because every tiny computer task has to be spelt out in detail in it, it is called a *low-level* language. Assembly language is not so low level, but it is still difficult for people to use. To further simplify programming, *high-level* languages were developed.

These are much more like ordinary human language, and each instruction in a high-level language embraces a large number of low-level language commands. It is therefore much quicker and easier to write programs in these languages than in low-level languages. Again, programs written in these languages have to be translated into assembly language, and from this into machine code.

Another advantage of high-level languages is the fact that they can be used on a variety of processors. The translation software looks after the job of converting them to the target assembly language(s). This means that software written in high-level languages can be run on a wide range of computers, with minimal changes. In practice, the situation is not as tidy as this, as many high-level languages differ somewhat from one machine to another. One of the worst offenders in this respect is the BASIC programming language which is popular on home computers. This has many 'dialects' with wide differences between them.

However, not all languages suffer in this way, and two which are used for business software and which are standard across a range of machines are COBOL and a language called 'C'.

3.2 System Software

System software is in two parts. First, there is the *operating system* or OS, which enables the computer to operate its various devices, like disk drives. Then there are a range of *utilities* which enable it to perform a number of subsidiary tasks like formatting disks, making backups of disks, and so on.

On IBM PC/ATs and compatible computers, the operating system is called *DOS*, short for 'disk operating system'. The version supplied on genuine IBM PCs is called PC-DOS, whereas compatibles use a version called MS-DOS. The 'MS' stands for Microsoft, the software house that wrote both versions of the OS. For all practical purposes, PC-DOS and MS-DOS are identical.

On IBM's PS/2 computers, the operating system is called OS/2; this offers more facilities than DOS, but is sufficiently like it to allow PS/2 machines to run PC/AT software.

If you use the BBC microcomputer in your college, note that its operating system is called *DFS*, short for 'disk filing system'.

Whichever computer you use, the operating system will carry out a standard range of tasks. These include accessing files on the disk, renaming files, copying files, deleting files, backing up complete disks, and so on. The most important task of all is running your application software. To tell the operating system to perform one of these tasks you have to issue a command. This is normally a word typed at the keyboard.

For example, to delete a file, the command is DEL, and so you type DEL followed by the name of the file. To copy a file you type COPY followed by the filename. And to run a file, you type just the filename.

There may by some variations in the commands used by different operating systems. On the BBC micro, for example, you have to type a '*' in front of the command. If you don't, that computer thinks you are trying to enter a command in the BASIC language instead of trying to address the operating system.

A major task of the operating system is to organise the storage of files on disk. It keeps a list of files and their locations in a part of the disk called the directory. To display a listing of these files you type the command DIR. (At least, this is the command used by DOS and some other operating systems. If you have BBC micros, the command is *CAT.) Some of the files listed will be software files, others will be files of data (or text or image) that you create yourself when you use the software. File names can by up to eight characters long on most systems (seven on the BBC micro).

Because of the large number of files that can be stored on a hard disk, an important task of the operating system is to allow you to split the list of their names into separate directories. For example, you might want to keep your word processing software and text files in one directory, your record keeping software and data files in a second directory, and so on. This helps you to keep your files in good order, so that it is easy to find files whose names you have forgotten, or to delete files that you no longer use.

These directories are organised in a tree-like structure. The main directory is called the *root* directory. This will normally contain a number of system files, but it also branches out to all the other directories. When you issue the command DIR to see what's in the root directory, a list of its files appears on the screen together with a list of the names of these other directories.

How do you look at the contents of another directory? You have to type a command telling the operating system to change its attention to that directory, and then type the command DIR. If you use DOS, the command to change directories is CD followed by the directory name.

To give an example of this, on my hard disk I have some record keeping and word processing software called Q&A, stored in a directory called QA. To list the files that comprise this software, I have to type the two commands:

CD QA
DIR

Just as branches on a tree split off into smaller branches, so directories on a disk can be split into subdirectories. For example, I keep text files created by the word processing part of Q&A in a subdirectory of the QA directory called TEXT, and the data files created by the record keeping part in a subdirectory called DATA. So when I issue the above commands I see listed on my screen not just the names of the files that comprise the QA directory, but also the subdirectory names TEXT and DATA.

Suppose I want to display a list of the files in the TEXT

subdirectory – you can probably work out for yourself the sequence of commands I have to type. They are:

CD TEXT
DIR

To access the files stored on a disk in a different drive, you have to tell the operating system to switch its attention to that drive. The floppy disk drive on a personal computer is called Drive A, and to access it you type the command:

A

If the computer has a second floppy disk drive, it is called Drive B. The hard disk, if there is one, is always Drive C, and to switch to it if the computer is currently accessing Drive A or B, you type the command:

C

There are many other operating system commands, and as I've said there are differences between the commands used by one type of computer and those of another. However, the above gives some idea of what's involved.

Most occasional users of computers find the operating system commands difficult to remember and rather awkward to use. Fortunately, it is possible to avoid making much use of the operating system. The reason is that application software often provides facilities for carrying out many of these tasks, and as well as this many computers nowadays provide the kind of environment software described below that gives a more 'friendly' approach to computing.

3.3   Environment Software

Environment software resides in the computer's RAM alongside the operating system, providing an easy-to-use and intuitive way of using the computer. Rank Xerox laid the foundation for this type of software back in the 1970s, when it carried out painstaking research into the way in which people interact with computers.

Pressing the arrow keys on the keyboard to move around the

screen, for instance, is not very efficient or natural, and so the mouse was developed. Pushing this across your desk produces corresponding movements of the cursor on the screen. Selecting files or software options by typing at the keyboard is also unnatural and inefficient, so a button is provided at the front of the mouse. Now, to make your selection, you merely push the mouse to move to the file or the option displayed on the screen, and click the button. In the case of a software program, you run it by 'double clicking', i.e. pressing the button twice in quick succession.

Xerox's research also showed that most people find the conventional text-based display unfriendly and difficult to use, preferring instead one that is graphics-based. In this, pictures or *icons* represent the functions and tasks of the system, examples being a picture of a wastepaper basket or 'trash can' to represent the delete function for getting rid of files, a filing drawer to represent a disk-drive, and so on. The cursor itself is represented by an icon, normally an arrow to point to files or functions.

Another feature of the environment that grew out of Xerox's research is the use of *windows*. A window is a rectangular area, superimposed on the rest of the screen, in which a menu of options is displayed, or another directory, or in which an application program is run. Used with the mouse, this type of screen display is very effective. Windows can be opened by clicking with the mouse, and options within them can be selected in the same way. Windows can be 'dragged' to other positions on the screen (by holding down the mouse button while moving it), and their size can be altered by dragging a corner.

The Apple Corporation was the first to apply Xerox's research commercially, when it brought out the Apple Macintosh in the mid-80s. Users of this computer are not aware of the operating system, as all interactions take place within the Macintosh operating environment. To run a piece of software, for example, you double click with the mouse on the icon that represents the software file.

The Macintosh environment proved very successful, and before long other implementations of Xerox's system were introduced for other computers. One that is similar to the Macintosh environment is GEM, produced by Digital Research Corporation, and this has been implemented on the PC, the Atari ST, and several others.

Apple Corporation took Digital Research to court over the similarities between GEM and the earlier Mac environment, and as a result Digital Research agreed to alter the implementation of GEM on the PC. The altered version of GEM appeared in October 1986, and this proved to be a pale shadow of the original implementation. Many people who use GEM in a serious way on the PC have kept to the original version.

Figure 3.1 shows a GEM display, with a window showing the contents of the GEMAPPS directory of the disk in Drive C. Note the slide bar at the right of the window, which you can use to scroll through the contents of the directory. The procedure is to 'point' to it with the mouse (i.e. move the arrow on the screen to it), hold down the mouse button, and 'drag' it to a new position. Other facilities include the list of menus at the top right of the screen, which are accessed by 'pointing' with the mouse. When they are accessed, a list of options 'pops up' in a window on the screen, which can be selected by pointing and clicking (see below).

Fig. 3.1   *A GEM display*

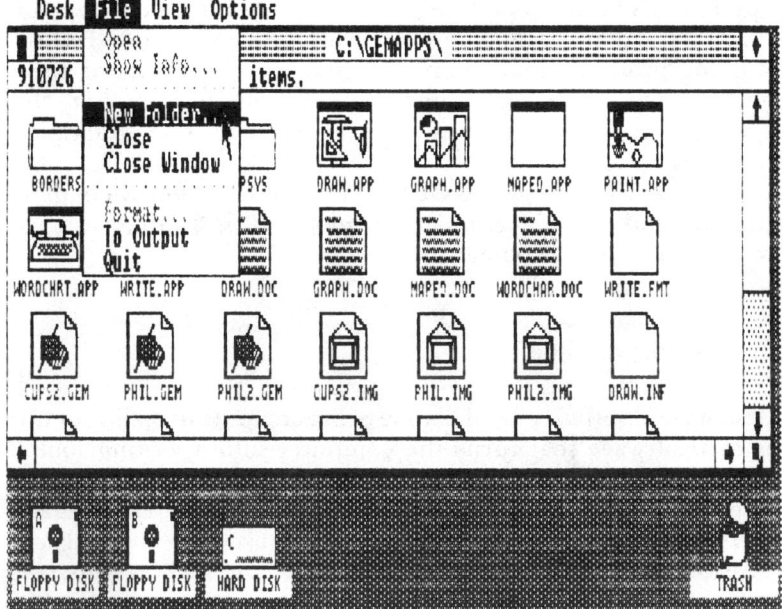

On the Mac, all applications programs run within its environment. This means that they use the features of the environment like the mouse, scroll bars, and pop-up windows. In the case of GEM, quite a number of programs are written to run within its environment. This not only means that users have the advantage of the mouse-and-windows environment, it also means that every piece of software handles in a similar way, cutting down the time it takes to learn them.

In the case of the PC, most applications will not run within the GEM environment. This means that when you select such an application within GEM (by clicking on its icon), it pushes GEM to one side and takes over the computer. It will then use its own ways of interacting with the user.

The other main operating environment, and potentially far more significant than the Mac/GEM environment, is Windows for the PC, produced by Microsoft. A version of Windows called Presentation Manager is the environment supplied with IBM's PS/2 computers. Windows operates in much the same way as the Mac/GEM environments, the main visible difference being that files are not represented by icons but instead are simply listed down the screen.

Windows' big advantage, however, is the *multi-tasking* capabilities that it offers. This means that you can run several applications at the same time, within different windows. So you can have a diary, a notebook, a word processor, your record-keeping program, and so on, all operational at the same time, and you are able to switch instantly from one to the other. Not only this, you can copy data or text created in one application into another.

Note that software such as GEM and Windows that provides these windows-and-mouse features is called *WIMP* software, short for 'window-icon-mouse-pointer'.

3.4   Application Software

Application software is, of course, what computing is all about. It is this software that turns the computer into a writing tool, a record-keeping tool, a diary, or whatever. Each piece of application software is a major program with many features, and it will normally be accompanied by a substantial manual and possibly also tutorial material on disk. As well as this, the software will probably consist of quite a number of programs supplied on several disks. The whole thing is called a *software package*.

There are many thousands of software packages on the market. It is reckoned that there are at least 2000 for the PC/AT alone. The competition is intense, and there are hundreds of word processing packages, for example, and hundreds of record-keeping packages. Most business packages cost between £100 and £500, depending on the features, and some types of package, such as computer-aided design packages, can cost several thousand pounds.

Today, many computers are used for office (i.e. 'business') applications, and the large number of business packages that there are available reflects this. There are plenty of other applications, and software for the drawing office and other areas of work abound. Here's a list of the main types of application software.

- Word processing, for writing letters, books, and other text-based documents.
- Desktop publishing, to create high-quality documents such as brochures and magazines incorporating a variety of typefaces and graphics.
- Presentation graphics, to create charts, notices, overhead transparencies, drawings, and other kinds of presentations.
- Record keeping, for storing, retrieving, and reporting on records of all types from personnel to stock.
- Spreadsheets, for manipulating tables of figures to produce quantitative analyses of data of all kinds, from cash-flow forecasts to statistical analyses.
- Computer-aided design (CAD), to enable professional draughtsmen to design offices, buildings, machines, circuit boards, and so on.
- Communications, to enable the computer to send data to and receive data from other computers over the telephone line or other communications links.
- Expert systems, to store the knowledge of a number of experts in a particular subject or 'domain', and to enable others to retrieve that knowledge in the form of advice on a particular set of circumstances within that domain.

Besides these major categories of software, there are other widely used types of package, including:

financial accounting;	ideas organisers or 'outliners';
project planning;	diary systems;
authoring languages of computer-based learning material;	route planning software for journeys;
statistical analysis;	business simulations;
	games.

On top of this there are software packages for controlling machine tools in the factory, chemical processes, warehousing systems, financial transactions, and many other industrial and commercial applications.

You will be introduced to a number of these packages in later chapters of this book. This section aims to give just an overall outline of what's available and the features of this type of software.

a) Menu-driven packages

Most software packages are *menu-driven*. This bit of computer jargon means that you make use of them by selecting options from a 'menu' presented on the screen. Menus often extend to several levels, so that having selected an option in one menu you will be presented with a subsidiary menu with several sub-options. Normally, though, you have to work through only two or three levels of menu to get to the facility you require.

For an example of this, look at Figure 3.2. It shows the main menu of a word processing and record-keeping package called Q&A. You select an option either by pressing the first letter of the option, or by moving the highlight bar down to that option (by pressing the spacebar or the down-arrow key) and pressing the ENTER key.

If you press 'W' to select the 'Write' word processing module from this menu, you are presented with the subsidiary menu shown in Figure 3.3. Most of the options on this menu will take you straight to the task you wish to perform – for example, pressing 'T' for Type/edit takes you to the word processing screen for creating a new piece of text. If you press 'U', however, you are taken to a further 'Utilities' menu shown in Figure 3.4.

Fig. 3.2   *The Q&A main menu*

```
┌─────────────────────────────────────────────┐
│                                             │
│              Q&A MAIN MENU                   │
│ ═══════════════════════════════════════════ │
│                                             │
│                                             │
│          F - File                           │
│          R - Report                         │
│          W - Write                          │
│          A - Assistant                      │
│          U - Utilities                      │
│          X - Exit Q&A                       │
│                                             │
│                                             │
└─────────────────────────────────────────────┘
```

Fig. 3.3 *The* Write *menu*

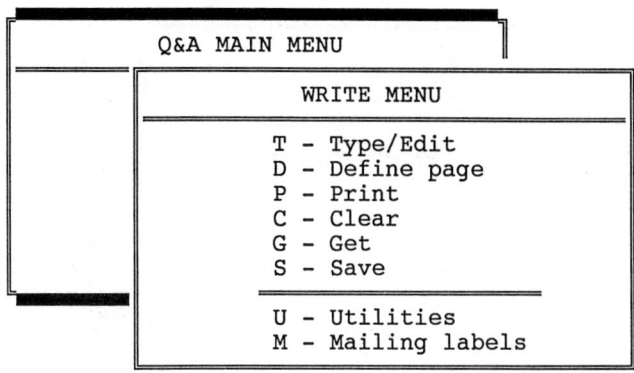

Fig. 3.4 *The* Utilities *menu*

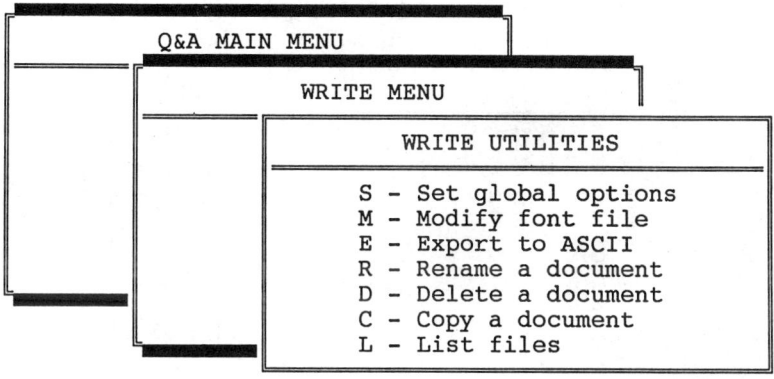

In the case of software that uses the window-icon-mouse-pointer (WIMP) method of working described earlier, the main menu will normally be permanently visible as a list across the top of the screen, and an option from it will be selected by using the mouse. (By 'pointing' to it and then 'clicking'.) The relevant sub-menu then appears in a window that 'pops up' (or 'pulls down') immediately below the selected option, and you select a sub-option from this by clicking again. GrandView, the package I normally use for writing books, works in this way, and Figure 3.5 shows a GrandView screen with the 'Print' menu selected.

Fig. 3.5 *The GrandView screen showing the* Print *pull-down menu*

```
File  Edit  Window  View  Reorganize  Print  Layout  Categories  Special      38k══1
A:\IT3

                                    P - Print...                        ♥P
                                    O - Print Options...
                                    S - Page Setup...
                                    T - Table of Contents...
                                    F - Font/Style By Level...
                                    H - Custom Headers/Footers...
                                    A - Auto Headers/Footers...
                                    R - Reveal Format Tags      F5
                                    L - Load Print Driver...
                                    B - Hard Page Break         ♥/
                                    C - Conditional Break...
                                    N - Insert Page Number
```

In the case of software
(WIMP) method of workin
menu will normally be p
across the top of the s
will be selected by usi
it and then 'clicking.)
appears in a window tha
immediately below the s
a sub-option from this
the package I normally
this way, and Figure 3.
the 'Print' menu select

Figure 3.5 The GrandView screen showing
            the 'Print' pull-down menu

If I select the first of the options in this print
menu (by clicking on 'Print...', a further window
shown in Figure 3.6 appears allowing me to select a
range of print settings (by clicking on the ones I

```
(Shft,♥Alt)        Print Current Outline        (F1=Help,ESC=Exit) 326k
```

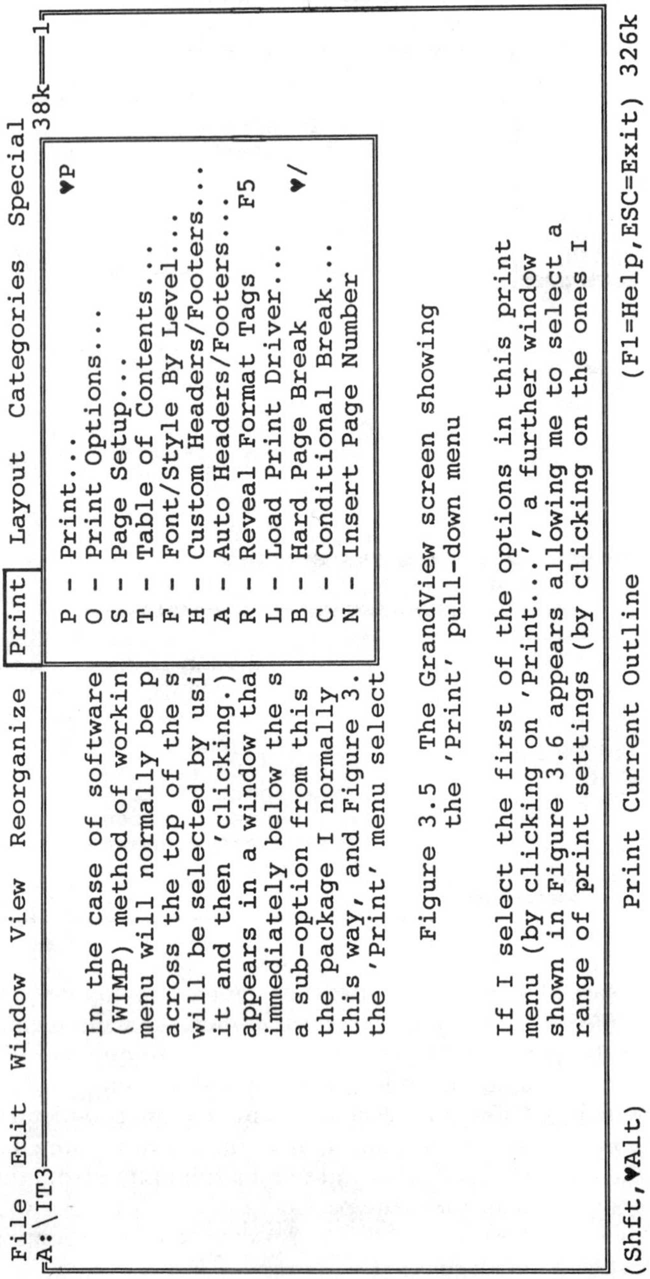

Fig. 3.6 *The* Print *dialogue box in GrandView*

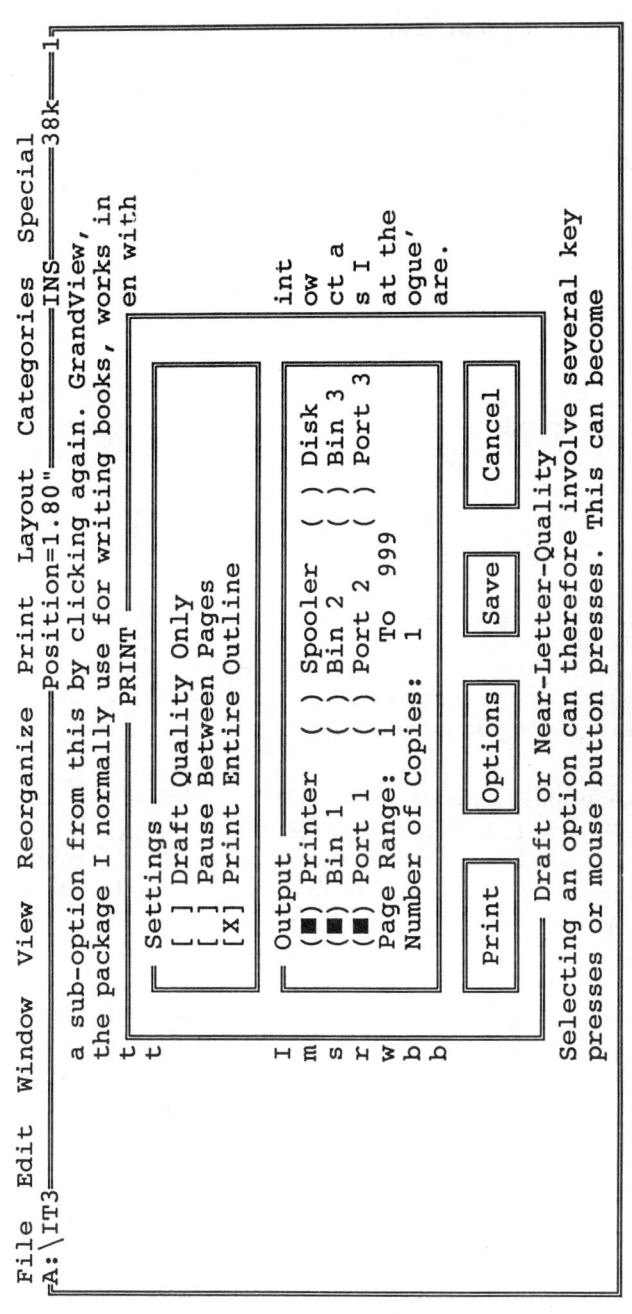

If I select the first of the options in this print menu (by clicking on 'Print . . .', a further window shown in Figure 3.6 appears allowing me to select a range of print settings (by clicking on the ones I want), and finally to click on the 'Print' box at the bottom to print my document. This kind of 'dialogue' box is commonly used in windows-and-mouse software.

Selecting an option can therefore involve several key presses or mouse button presses. This can become tedious for frequently-used options, and so most packages provide short-cuts. These normally involve holding down the CTRL or ALT keys and pressing another key. For example, to bypass the print menus in GrandView I hold down the ALT key and press 'P'.

b) Macros

Most packages also provide a *macro* facility allowing you to set up your own short-cut key presses. Using this, you can record and store on disk long sequences of key presses, to be played back at the touch of a 'hot key' – ALT or CTRL plus another key.

This can be a great time saver. When I start a new chapter in this book, for example, I press a single key which:

- loads the necessary labelling style to produce the section numbering, etc;
- sets the line length and other page formatting;
- sets up the page numbering;
- performs other background tasks.

This all happens instantaneously and automatically, and I know that it will make the final printed result look exactly right on the page. Of course, I had to set up the macro in the first place, which took several minutes, but that was time well spent since I can now use it time and time again.

c) On-screen help

Most application packages provide a large number of facilities, and it is difficult to remember how to use them all. This is especially so if you are a new or infrequent user. Referring to the manual can be tedious and time-consuming, so the package normally provides on-screen help. You merely have to press the 'help' key – usually the function key marked F1 – and a screen of help appears.

This help will normally be context-sensitive, i.e. it will relate to your current task, and there may be menu options included in it to allow you to jump quickly to other screens of related help.

d) Command-driven software

Some software is *command-driven*. This means that to use one of its facilities you have to type a command instead of selecting from a menu. This kind of software is more difficult to use than the menu-driven variety, but it does allow you a great deal of flexibility and power in your use of it. For example, you can string commands together to create a program, which when run will carry out a large number of tasks automatically.

This type of software is mainly restricted to record-keeping packages, of which dBase III is the best-known example. The programming capabilities of dBase are such that you can use it to set up systems for handling accounts and other specialist tasks in a menu-driven way, and users can run these without needing to know anything about dBase itself. In fact, a large number of specialist applications are produced in this way by professional dBase programmers and sold commercially.

Most command-driven packages also provide an option which provides menus for those who want them, and dBase III is no exception. However, if your needs are such that you do not make use of the software's programming capabilities (and most people don't), you are probably better off using a simpler package such as Q&A, which is designed to be run via menus. Although these simpler packages lack some of the power and features of complex products such as dBase, they are much easier to learn and use, and therefore more suitable for many applications.

e) Screen modes

Most computers provide a number of screen modes. In the case of word-processing and record-keeping applications, for example, an 80-column screen mode is best. This means that each horizontal line across the screen displays up to 80 characters, which matches exactly the width of a piece of paper. However, if you are using a colour monitor, it must have a good resolution to display the characters clearly.

Sometimes a 40-column screen display will be used, a notable example being the BBC microcomputer with its 40-column Mode 7 'Teletext' screen mode. This screen mode is far from ideal for word processing, as it does not allow you to see much text at a time (about a fifth of an A4 page, in fact), and the arrangement of the text on the screen will be nothing like what's printed out on paper. The advantage, however, is that the characters are so large that you can use a cheap low-resolution colour monitor with this screen mode.

Almost all application packages on personal computers use 80-column screen modes.

3.5 Software for Office Automation

During the last decade, information technology has had a greater impact on the world of the office than on any other human activity. The main reason for this is that the office has had a great deal of catching up to do in terms of automation and productivity, and it is only since the arrival of the personal computer that this has become possible.

Factory automation has been with us for many decades. We are used to the idea of business spending large amounts of money on major items of factory equipment in order to improve productivity. Office work, in contrast to factory work, is much more varied, with many relatively small jobs to be done, such as writing letters, some filing, sending out memos, and so on. It is just not cost-effective to apply large computers to small tasks like these. (There are, though, some large-scale routine office jobs in big organisations, such as the payroll, stock control, and accounts, and mainframe computers have been used for these since the 1950s.)

The small-scale nature of the work demands low-cost computing facilities, which is why office automation had to await the development of cheap personal computers. That's the reason why it is the office that has benefitted most from the silicon chip revolution, and why most serious personal computer software is aimed at the office worker.

For most of this decade the main office automation packages have been word processing, record keeping, spreadsheets, graphics in the form of charts and graphs, and communications. Recently desktop publishing and presentation graphics software have been developed, though these can be considered as extensions of word processing and graphics software rather than anything radically new. Add to these a few other types of software package such as diary systems and outliners, and a few devices such as facsimile and modems (which are discussed later) and you have encompassed most of the office automation scene.

Because of the importance of office automation software, and because this is a book aimed at business and commerce students (rather than, say, engineers), we shall be covering it in some depth in the next chapters.

3.6 Integrated Software

It's worth pointing out that quite a number of *integrated* packages are available. These aim to cover most of the requirements of office automation in a single package, with modules for word processing, record keeping, spreadsheets, graphics, and communications. The advantages to the user of an integrated package is that if you require all these functions:

- it provides them at lower cost than if you bought a number of separate packages;
- all the modules will have similar ways of working, so that once you have learned one it is not so difficult to master the others;
- all the modules will be file-compatible, meaning, for example, that a file of data created by the record-keeping module can be loaded into the spreadsheet, so that you can manipulate and display it as a table of data.

The disadvantages are that an individual module – such as the word-processing or the record-keeping module – will not be as powerful as a separate package that is dedicated to those tasks; and if you only need one or two modules then an integrated package is probably more expensive than buying separate packages.

Integrated software is not quite so attractive today as it was a few years ago, and most users tend to opt for stand-alone dedicated packages. One reason for the continued popularity of the latter is that the main advantages of integrated software – common ways of working, and file compatibility within modules – are now shared by many stand-alone packages. Software packages generally are conforming more and more to standard ways of working (such as the windows-and-mouse environment), and many of them provide facilities to convert their files to standard formats for loading into other software.

I shall be describing some of the packages that are available in the next chapter.

Questions

1 Give two advantages and one disadvantage of using WIMP software.
2 Environment software such as GEM and Windows is becoming increasingly popular on PCs and ATs. Give two advantages of this type of software, and try to think of one disadvantage.
3 Explain why personal computers have had their greatest impact on the world of the office.

Chapter 4
Writing and Publishing with Computers

A major reason for the increasing use of computers in the office is to speed up the writing process. Whether it's memos, reports, letters, books, legal documents, brochures, magazines, or just jotting down and organising a list of ideas – computers make the job easier and quicker. Besides this, the quality of the finished result is much better, provided a suitable printer is used.

In most offices, replacing typewriters by computers running word processing software will approximately double the output of written work. There are a number of reasons for this increased productivity, including the following:

- you can make alterations on the screen, so avoiding the need to retype whole pages;
- information which is repeatedly used, such as standard paragraphs in legal documents, or names and addresses in letters, can be stored on disk and automatically inserted in the document.

The improved quality of the final result is partly because alterations and corrections are made on the screen, so consigning to history the use of Tippex and overtyping on the paper. It is also due to the writing aids that may accompany the word processing software:

- spell checkers, i.e. dictionaries of 100 000 words or more, stored on disk, which enable you to quickly check the spelling of individual words or all the words in a document;
- thesauruses, i.e. dictionaries of alternative words, to help you express your meaning more precisely and to add variety to your writing;
- style checkers, i.e. software which will analyse your documents and make suggestions for improving your style.

Not only this, but outlining software is available which will help you organise your thoughts and ideas into neat and helpful synopses from which to work. And, when you have finished writing your material with a word processor, you can print it from a desktop publishing package. This will transform it into a classy piece of work with large headlines, a variety of typefaces, and pictures and other graphics effects.

I've mentioned already that I am using a package called GrandView to write this book. This is a combined outliner and word processor. It enables me to carry out the entire composition process, from organising the outline of a chapter to writing the material in each section, in one smooth operation. Then, when I've finished writing my material, I press a 'hot-key' to activate a macro which instantly converts it to a format for desktop publishing (DTP) using the Ventura DTP package described later.

This chapter deals with these software aids to writing. Before we begin, it's worth pointing out that the distinction between outliners, word processors, and DTP software is gradually disappearing. A number of modern word processors are providing outlining and DTP capabilities, and desktop publishing packages are now providing more in the way of word processing features. Increasingly over the next few years, you will be able to use the same software for all three jobs.

I'll start by looking at word processing (WP) software, then I'll describe outliners, and finally DTP software.

4.1 Word Processing

Suppose you decide to produce one of your college assignments on an ordinary typewriter. There are a number of decisions and tasks that you will have to undertake.

- You will have to decide on the size of the margins at the left, right, top, and bottom of the page. You will also have to decide where to put the page number, and whether you will type your assignment in single line spacing, one-and-a-half line spacing, or double spacing. All these are part of the *format* of your page. Having decided the format, you will then make the necessary adjustments on the typewriter to implement it. If you change your mind half-way through, you will have to retype everything that you have done so far.
- You will have to produce a complete (handwritten) draft of your work before you begin typing, making any editorial changes on this. This is because it is very difficult to make

changes once a word or sentence has been typed on the paper.

- You will then have to type your draft, and any mistakes in your typing will involve laborious corrections involving Tippex and retyping.
- If you want to do anything a little out of the ordinary, such as centring a heading, you will have to laboriously count the number of words in the heading, and then work out where on the line you will have to begin typing it.
- Many things that you might want to do to enhance the appearance of your work are impossible with an ordinary typewriter. For example, you can't justify the right edges of each line so that they all line up (like the right-hand edges of the lines on this page).

You might have an electronic typewriter, which has chips inside it to overcome some of these problems. For example, it will have a facility to delete the last few characters that you have typed before printing them on the paper, so allowing you to correct your typing. It will also provide automatic justification and centring.

Nevertheless, you will still have to produce a draft of your work before you begin, because your electronic typewriter probably won't allow you to change whole sentences and paragraphs, or to alter the format of your page once you have started. It will also lack many of the other word processing features described in this section.

Word processing software on a computer revolutionises your whole approach to writing, and speeds up and improves your work enormously. Here are a few examples.

If you type a paragraph, and want to change part of it, that's no problem: you zip back with the arrow keys or the mouse, delete a few words here and there, and type in your revisions. Or perhaps you want to move the entire paragraph somewhere else: you simply mark its beginning and end, move to the point in your text where you want it to go, press a key, and it's instantly moved.

If, having printed your work, you don't like its appearance but wish to change the margins, or centre the page number at the foot of the page instead of printing it at the top left, or alter the line spacing, this is no problem either. You simply press a few keys to carry out the necessary changes on the screen, and then print again.

If you have used a word often throughout your text, let's say the word 'microcomputer', and you wish to change all occurrences of it to another word, say 'computer', you can do so at a stroke. Just press a key to call up the software's search-and-replace facility, type the word that you wish to search for (microcomputer), and the word that you wish to replace it with (computer), press a key to carry out the operation, and within a few seconds the job's done.

Fig. 4.1   *Advert for the Write Now package*

WRITE NOW
THE INTUITIVE SOFTWARE
The Intuitive Word Processing Software

Write Now is the word processing system designed with the business professional in mind. Every element in **Write Now** is meant to save you time in learning, writing, correcting – in everything it takes to produce a business letter, memo, or report.

Take **Write Now** out of the box. Place it in the disk drive and type "now". The program *and* dictionary will load into memory. You start typing *immediately*. There's no installation procedure with **Write Now**. No copy protection. No bag full of floppy disks. No wait.

Corrects Spelling As You Type
Write Now highlights misspellings as you type – you don't need a separate spell-checking program. Mistakes are highlighted in inverse video the instant they occur. Or, you can spell-check the entire document when you're through typing. The choice is yours.

Spelling Suggestions are available. You can ask for them at any time, or have them pop up automatically the instant a misspelling occurs. Scroll down to the correct word and insert it into the text with a single keystroke.

Write Now will even complete words for you, saving you keystrokes and time. Type "fj" and – with **Clairvoyance** switched on – **Write Now** will automatically add "ord" to make the word "fjord."

You can even prevent misspellings from happening. With **Spell Guard** on, only correctly-spelled words can appear on the screen.

Powerful Word Processing
Write Now puts advanced word processing features at your fingertips using on-screen menus or speed key commands.

Features include:
- Automatic Paragraph Reformatting
- Full text justification
- Headers and Footers
- Page Numbering
- Page Breaks
- Mail Merge
- Saves files in ASCII
- Advanced File Management
- Not copy protected
- Single disk operation
- Cut and Paste
- Search and Replace
- Supports common printers; easily add your own
- File Merge
- Insert or overwrite mode
- Enhance text: bold, underline, custom printer enhancements, fonts, subscripts, superscripts, etc.
- Expandable 35,000 word dictionary
- Context-sensitive help always available
- Free telephone support for registered customers
  . . . and more

Figure 4.1 shows an advert for a package called Write Now, listing the kinds of features that WP offers. Many of these features and the way in which they are used are described in this chapter. To begin with, there are a few word processing concepts that you need to know.

4.2   Word Processing Concepts

The ideas that you should be familiar with in word processing include the following:

a) Editing screen
This refers to the screen display on which you create and edit your text. It will be 80 characters wide on most computer systems, which exactly matches the width of the (A4) page that you will be printing on. However, it will only be 25 lines deep, which is less than half the length of an A4 page if single spacing is used. Not all of these lines will be available for your document, as one or two lines at the top or bottom of the screen will be taken up with a list of menu options or other messages.

b) Cursor
Your position on the editing screen, i.e. the point at which the next character you type will appear, is marked by a character-sized block called the text cursor. For greater emphasis, it will normally flash, i.e. alternate between the foreground and background colours. If you wish to edit some earlier text, you move this cursor to the editing point, using the arrow keys or other special keys such as PgUp and PgDn.

In the case of WIMP (window-icon-mouse-pointer) software, there will be a second *mouse cursor*. To help you distinguish it from the text cursor, it will have a different shape, typically an arrow. The mouse cursor allows you to pick menu options and perform other tasks without losing your place in the text. Another advantage is the speed and ease with which the mouse allows you to move around your text for editing. You push it to bring the mouse cursor to the editing point, then click the mouse button to update the text cursor to that point.

c) Scrolling
If your document is more than half a page long, it will not fit onto the computer screen. As you add to it, your earlier words will disappear at the top. To recall them from apparent oblivion, you have to *scroll* the text back down the screen (so that your later words disappear at the foot of the screen). You can do this by using the arrow keys or other cursor-movement keys to run the text cursor up the screen. In the case of WIMP software, you can scroll by moving the mouse cursor to the scroll bar at the side of the screen, then holding down the mouse button.

d) Block operation
Often you need to carry out an operation on a whole block of
text, such as a number of words, sentences, or paragraphs. You
may want to delete them, move them elsewhere in the text, or
copy them into a separate file on disk for use in other documents.
The procedure is to mark the block in some way, and then press
the key that carries out the required function. Exactly how this is
done depends upon your word processing software package.

If you are not using WIMP software, the procedure is to:

- move the cursor (with the arrow or other cursor-movement
  keys) to the start of the block;
- then press a special block marking key (which might be one of
  the function keys or alternatively CTRL and a key, depending
  on the software);
- then move the cursor to the end of the block and press the
  block-marking key again;
- if you wish to delete the block, you will normally then press
  the DEL key, and if you want to move it elsewhere in your text
  you will move the cursor to the new position and press
  whichever key your software uses for block movements; alternatively you may wish to copy the block, i.e. make a duplicate
  of it in the new position, or copy out to a separate file on disk,
  in which case other keys will be used.

In the case of WIMP software, the procedure to mark a block is to
move the mouse cursor to the start of the block and then 'drag'
the mouse across the block to the end. This involves holding
down the mouse button while you move the mouse cursor across
the block, the software highlighting the text you are marking.
Then you press one of the special keys to delete, move, or copy
the block.

e) Insert and overtype
When typing, you can be in either *insert* or *overtype* mode. The
main difference is this: when you are typing new words in the
middle of some existing text in insert mode, the subsequent
words are pushed along; if you are working in overtype mode,
however, the new words go over and replace the old words.

Most people prefer to work in insert mode. With most software
you switch between modes by pressing the INS key at the bottom
right of the keyboard.

f) Wordwrap
When you use an ordinary typewriter, you have to operate the

carriage return at the end of each line. With word processing software, when the cursor reaches the end of one line it automatically moves to the start of the next. Furthermore, to avoid splitting words in half at the end of a line, it will move the last word to the new line. This means that you can forget about line ends when typing with word processing software, as the computer looks after everything.

This feature – moving words to a new line that would otherwise be chopped in two – is called *wordwrap*.

g) WYSIWYG

This isn't a creepy-crawly, it stands for 'What You See Is What You Get'. In other words, what you see on the screen is what will be printed out on paper. Most word processing packages are WYSIWYG so far as page formatting is concerned – i.e. they will show where each line ends, the size of the margins, the page breaks, and so on.

Few packages, however, show different typefaces and styles on the screen – such as italics, different sizes of type, and so on. In the case of the PC/AT, effects such as italics may be shown by colours. More graphically-oriented screen displays, such as those on the Apple Mac, are able to show these effects much more easily, and WP packages for these machines are fully WYSIWYG.

(In defence of the PC/AT, it should be pointed out that for most WP jobs there is little advantage in being able to show italics, etc. on the screen, and the PC/AT is supported by a much wider range of software. My favourite word processor – Grand-View – is only available on this machine. It's also worth pointing out that desktop publishing software, in contrast to WP software on the PC/AT, is fully WYSIWYG, showing all effects as they will be printed.)

h) Mailmerge

You are probably familiar with the idea of *mailmerge* from the personalised mailshots that you receive from organizations like Reader's Digest. These are produced by merging some standard text produced on a word processor with names and addresses and perhaps other data held on a record-keeping package.

Mailmerge is used by many organisations to promote their products by means of what they call 'direct mailings' (and what we might call junk mail). Many modern WP packages, especially those that are part of an integrated package with a record-keeping module, enable this kind of task to be carried out very easily.

i) Boilerplating

This term refers to the technique of making up documents by 'bolting together' standard paragraphs stored on disk. Many legal documents, for example, are produced in this way, giving substantial savings in time and labour. Depending on the WP package, you can do this either by loading in the paragraphs one after another onto the editing screen, or else inserting in the master document the names under which the standard paragraphs are filed.

j) Menu

I've described menus and menu-driven software already (Chapter 3), but I mention it again here because word processing software is always menu-driven. This means that you select its various functions from a menu of choices that is either listed across the top or bottom of the screen or else appears in a window. Often, the package will provide short-cuts to many of these options by pressing either a function key or CTRL or ALT and a key. Also, you can normally set up your own macros to carry out frequent jobs.

4.3   How to Go About Word Processing

Although word processors differ somewhat in terms of the facilities they offer, and they may differ quite a lot in the way in which these facilities are used, they all do much the same job. They allow you to write, alter, format, save, and print documents such as memos, letters, and college assignments. Your general approach to this task does not vary, whichever package you use, and is described below.

a) Outline your text

First, you should produce an outline of your document. This will normally be a list of headings and sub-headings, with perhaps some notes entered under each. If you are very good at writing, you may be able to produce this in your head, reorganising it mentally and holding it in your mind while you produce your work on the word processor. Most people, however, need to write down their outline, especially if the document is fairly substantial like a college assignment.

Your outline can be written longhand on paper, or else typed into the computer using the kind of outlining software described later. The advantage of the latter is that it enables you to reorganise your ideas very easily. In the case of a word processor with outlining facilities, you can produce your outline on the editing screen, and then key in the text below each heading. If you then reorganise your outline by moving headings around, the associated text moves as well.

b) Create your text

Normally, you will decide your page formatting – line length, etc. – before you begin, even if you simply accept the default settings offered by the package. However, you can change your mind at any time, and your work so far will be automatically and instantly reformatted to the new settings. The procedure for setting the page format varies from package to package.

When you start, the cursor will be positioned at the top left of the screen, and you enter your text just as if you were typing on a clean sheet of paper. If you make a mistake, you can delete the last few characters by pressing the backspace key towards the top right of the keyboard, and retype. The software will look after the ends of lines, and the only time you need to press the ENTER key (equivalent to the carriage return on a typewriter) is between paragraphs, when you should press it twice to insert a blank line.

Provided you insert blank lines between paragraphs, you don't need to indent the first line of a paragraph. (This book doesn't have blank lines between paragraphs, so the first line of each paragraph is indented.) If you want an indent, you normally produce it by pressing the TAB key at the left of the keyboard.

c) Edit your text

You will certainly need to make alterations to the text you have typed. This is not only to correct typing errors, but also to reorganise sentences and paragraphs, and to insert new material that comes to mind.

The arrow keys will move you a character at a time in the obvious direction (up, down, left, or right), and CTRL held down while tapping an arrow key will normally move you by bigger amounts, e.g. a word at a time to the left or right. Larger jumps are also possible, e.g. CTRL with Home key will normally take you to the start of the document, and CTRL-End will take you to the end. Better still at moving around is the mouse, if you have WIMP software.

The DEL key will delete the character at the cursor position, whereas the backspace key will delete the previous character. Your software will also provide special keys to delete a word at a time, or whole lines. The mouse also provides an excellent method of deleting, by 'dragging' it across the block you wish to delete, and pressing DEL or the backspace key.

Most WP software provides an 'undo' facility to put back any material that you have deleted in error – invaluable when you are carrying out block operations. Other facilities that I've mentioned earlier are also available, including block copy, block move, and search-and-replace.

The best-known word processing package is WordStar. (Best-known not because it is the best, but, because it has been around such a long time, it has become a standard. It is available on a wide range of computers, and it has been adopted by many businesses for their WP work.) WordStar uses various combinations of CTRL plus another key to carry out all of its editing tasks and menu options. I mention this because a number of other software packages offer the WordStar ways of working as an alternative to their own, and it is useful to be familiar with its main key combinations.

Most of WordStar's control keys are logically organised, designed to be accessed by the right hand with the little finger on CTRL and another finger on the other key. If you use WordStar in your college, your tutor will provide a handout listing the key combinations that you need to know.

d) Save your text

Normally, you will want to save onto disk the document you have produced. This may be because you have not finished it and wish to return to it later, or because you think you may want to use all or part of it on a future occasion. Your word processing package will provide a 'save' option, and all you have to do is supply a suitable file name. This name should be something meaningful, so that you can easily locate your file later on from the dozens stored on the disk.

If you are producing a long document, it's worth re-saving it from time to time as you work, in case disaster strikes such as a power failure. This is very unlikely to happen, of course, but it's good practice to save your work every half-an-hour or so, to ensure that you never lose too much. Also, you should keep backup copies of your files on floppy disks which are stored away from the computer, in case of more serious disasters such as fire.

Some word processing packages will automatically save to disk every few minutes to guard against loss of work. GrandView does this, and I have set its 'autosave' facility to operate every 30 minutes. That way I can forget about the problem.

e) Print your text

The 'print' facility on your word processing package will provide a number of printing options. These may include specifying the line spacing, switching justification off or on, printing in columns, and printing just a selection of pages from your document instead of all of it. Once you have made the appropriate selections from what's on offer, you can press the appropriate key to send your work to the printer. But make sure that it is switched on and connected to the computer!

Your package will also allow you to select alternative printer drivers from the range that it supplies. If you are printing to an Epson FX80 or compatible printer, for example, you must select the Epson FX80 driver. If you use the wrong driver, then emboldening, underlining, and other enhancements will not work, and in some cases complete garbage may be printed instead of your masterpiece.

f) Other facilities

Word processors provide many other facilities besides those that I've mentioned here. To give you an idea of what's available, look at Figure 4.2. This shows the editing 'help' screen from Q&A, which is an easy-to-use word-processing and record-keeping package. You will notice, for example, that you can:

- perform calculations on any rows and columns of numbers that you type into your document (ALT-F9);
- call up document statistics such as the number of words (CTRL-F3);
- go straight to a particular page and line (CTRL-F7).

Fig. 4.2 *Some of the editing facilities of Q&A Write, listed in its editing* help *screen*

F1	Ctrl F1	Check spelling (word)	F2	Ctrl F2	Print text block		
	Shift F1	Check spelling (doc)		Shift F2	Use macros		
	F1	Info		F2	Print document		
F3	Ctrl F3	Document statistics	F4	Ctrl F4	Delete to end of line		
				Shift F4	Delete line (Ctrl Y)		
	F3	Delete block		F4	Delete word (Ctrl T)		
F5	Alt F5	Move block to file	F6	Alt F6	Hyphenate		
	Ctrl F5	Copy block to file		Ctrl F6	Define Page		
	Shift F5	Move block		Shift F6	Enhance text		
	F5	Copy block		F6	Set temporary margins		
F7	Alt F7	List fields	F8				
	Ctrl F7	Go to page/line		Ctrl F8	Export document		
	Shift F7	Restore text		Shift F8	Save document		
	F7	Search & Replace		F8	Options Menu		
F9	Alt F9	Calculate	F10				
	Ctrl F9	Make font assignments					
	Shift F9	Scroll screen down					
	F9	Scroll screen up		F10	Continue		

Esc-Cancel   PgDn-More

Another facility provided by most word processors is an export option, which allows you to save your text in a standard format that can be read by other software. The most widely-used format is ASCII, mentioned in Chapter 1. A further facility enables the word processor to *import* such files.

To give an example of these facilities, a text file exported in ASCII from a word processor on the BBC microcomputer can be sent by a communications link to a PC, and then imported into a PC word processor such as Q&A (see the next chapter for more details).

4.4   Outlining Software

Outlining packages, also called 'ideas organisers', allow you to organise entries into a hierarchical list of headings. These might be tasks to be done, topics to be covered in an assignment, names and addresses, or other textual information. This hierarchy is called an *outline*, and the headings that it contains are called *headlines*. You can have major headlines, sub-headlines, sub-sub-headlines, and so on.

Figure 4.3 shows the headlines in this chapter, produced in GrandView. The main headline is the name of the chapter, then at the next level come the sub-headlines (the section names), then at a lower level come the smaller topics. The labels 4.1, 4.2, a), b), etc. are automatically applied by the software to the headlines. Many labelling styles are possible in GrandView – I've selected this one merely because it is the style required for Chambers Commerce Series.

Fig. 4.3   *Outline of this chapter, produced in GrandView*

4 WRITING AND PUBLISHING WITH COMPUTERS
  4.1 Word Processing
  4.2 Word Processing
    Concepts
    a) Editing screen
    b) Cursor
    c) Scrolling
    d) Block operation
    e) Insert and overtype
    f) Wordwrap
    g) WYSIWYG
    h) Mailmerge
    i) Boilerplating
    j) Menu
  4.3 How to Go About Word
    Processing
    a) Outline your text
    b) Create your text
    c) Edit your text
    d) save your text
    e) Print your text
    f) Other facilities
  4.4 Outlining Software
  4.5 Desktop Publishing
  4.6 Creating a Publication
  4.7 Formatting Your Text

In an outliner such as GrandView, you can easily shuffle headlines around. You can promote headlines to a higher level, or demote them to a lower level, and so quickly reorganise your information. You can collapse (i.e. hide) low-level headlines, so that you can get an instant overview of your main headings, and immediately expand them again when you want a more detailed view.

You can also insert text below any headline – a few notes, or a substantial document such as this section of Chapter 4 that I am writing now. You can collapse this text, so that it does not get in the way of the rest of the outline, and you can instantly expand it again. Figure 4.3 is in fact a print-out of this chapter with all the text collapsed.

You can use outliners for any kind of task involving structured textual information, including the following:

- developing the outline of a report or a task. You can enter major headings, then break these down into subheadings, insert additional headings or subheadings at any time, and easily rearrange the outline until you have marshalled your thoughts into order;
- keeping a file of names, addresses, and telephone numbers. In this file, the names might be the main headings, with the addresses and phone numbers forming subsidiary text. Normally, you will collapse this text, so that only a list of names is visible. The software allows you to add new names and addresses at any time, to sort the list into alphabetical order, and to quickly locate individual names using the software's 'search' facility;
- keeping a diary. Major headings will be the names of the months, and subheadings will be days, labelled 1, 2, 3, etc. up to 30 or 31. Diary entries can be made either as text below these subheadings, or as sub-subheadings;
- maintaining a 'to-do' list for tasks that are not tied to a particular time and so do not fit into your diary. For this application you will probably have two main headings, namely 'To do' and 'Done'. New tasks are added under the first heading, and completed tasks are moved from the first heading to the second.

A sophisticated outliner like GrandView allows you to display several outlines on the screen at the same time in separate windows. Figure 4.4 shows part of my diary, address book, to-do list, and other outlines displayed in this way.

Fig. 4.4 *Several applications displayed in GrandView*

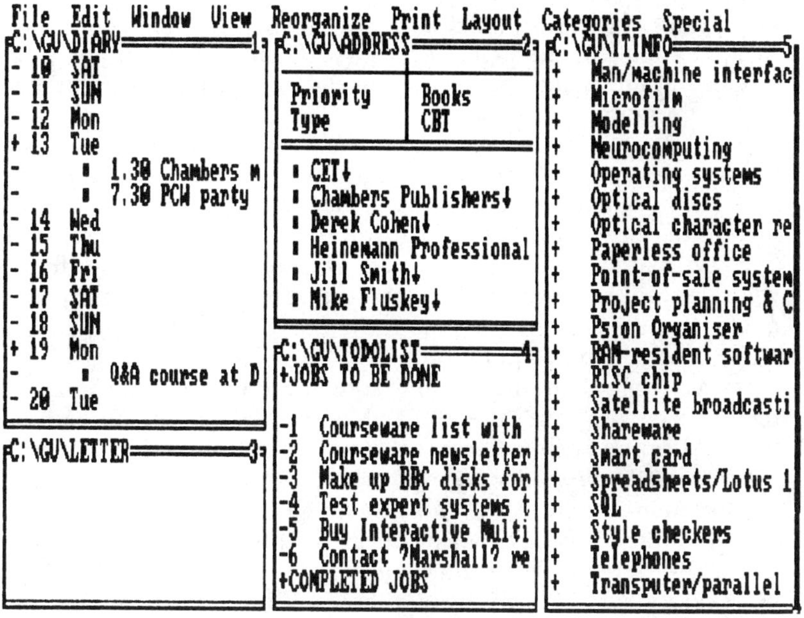

```
File  Edit  Window  View  Reorganize  Print  Layout  Categories  Special
┌C:\GV\DIARY════════════1┐┌C:\GV\ADDRESS═══════════2┐┌C:\GV\ITINFO══════════════5┐
│- 10  SAT              ││                         ││ +  Man/machine interfac  │
│- 11  SUN              ││ Priority   │ Books      ││ +  Microfilm             │
│- 12  Mon              ││ Type       │ CBT        ││ +  Modelling             │
│+ 13  Tue              ││                         ││ +  Neurocomputing        │
│-     ■  1.30 Chambers M││ ■ CET↓                 ││ +  Operating systems     │
│-     ■  7.30 PCW party ││ ■ Chambers Publishers↓ ││ +  Optical discs         │
│- 14  Wed              ││ ■ Derek Cohen↓          ││ +  Optical character re  │
│- 15  Thu              ││ ■ Heinemann Professional││ +  Paperless office      │
│- 16  Fri              ││ ■ Jill Smith↓           ││ +  Point-of-sale system  │
│- 17  SAT              ││ ■ Mike Fluskey↓         ││ +  Project planning & C  │
│- 18  SUN              │└─────────────────────────┘│ +  Psion Organiser       │
│+ 19  Mon              │┌C:\GV\TODOLIST═════════4┐ │ +  RAM-resident softwar  │
│-     ■  Q&A course at D││+JOBS TO BE DONE        │ │ +  RISC chip             │
│- 20  Tue              ││                        │ │ +  Satellite broadcasti  │
│                       ││-1  Courseware list with│ │ +  Shareware             │
┌C:\GV\LETTER══════════3┐│-2  Courseware newsletter│ │ +  Smart card            │
│                       ││-3  Make up BBC disks for│ │ +  Spreadsheets/Lotus 1  │
│                       ││-4  Test expert systems t│ │ +  SQL                   │
│                       ││-5  Buy Interactive Multi│ │ +  Style checkers        │
│                       ││-6  Contact ?Marshall? re│ │ +  Telephones            │
│                       ││+COMPLETED JOBS         │ │ +  Transputer/parallel   │
└───────────────────────┘└────────────────────────┘ └──────────────────────────┘
```

GrandView, as I've said, is a combined outliner and word processor. Other word processors incorporate outlining facilities, for example WordPerfect, which is the most popular word processor of all, and Word, which is Microsoft's major word processor. WordPerfect and Word offer more WP features than GrandView, but they are much less able as outliners.

4.5 Desktop Publishing

For simple publishing tasks, any word processor will do. You can design a form or a simple magazine using a WP package, and print it out on a daisy-wheel printer for use as a master for offset litho or photocopying. For anything beyond the simplest of publications, however, a WP package has severe limitations:

● it cannot produce the variety of typefaces that are possible with conventional typesetting and which you see in newspapers and magazines;

- it cannot incorporate in the document any pictures or other graphics, apart from a few simple effects;

- it does not give you complete control over the final appearance of the printed page (you can't, for example, put one paragraph in a box at the top right of the page, with other text organised around it).

Publishing using personal computers only became possible in the mid-1980s, when the price of laser printers fell to an affordable level. The significance of laser printers for DTP is the fact that, like dot matrix printers, they can produce text and graphics, whereas unlike dot matrix printers, they can produce a very high quality result. An added bonus is the fact that they are very fast and almost silent in operation.

It was Apple Computers that first realised the potential of laser printers. At the time, the Apple Mac was struggling to gain a toe-hold in the business computing scene. Although it offered a much better screen display than the PC/AT, and an excellent WIMP environment, this kind of capability had little relevance for the kind of things that business people wanted to do with their computers. A graphics-oriented task like publishing, however, would benefit from the Mac, and so Apple forged ahead to bring DTP into being.

Together with a company called Adobe, Apple brought out the Postscript page description language, which is a piece of software that enables computers to describe to laser printers and other typesetting equipment what the printed page should look like. Another company called Aldus brought out PageMaker, a software package that enabled Apple Macintosh users to 'make up' pages on the screen, i.e. insert text and graphics material and organise its layout ready for printing.

With this, the DTP revolution was born, and, being way ahead of the rest of the industry, Apple achieved its aim of getting Macs accepted as serious business machines.

There are, today, a variety of page make-up packages, running not only on the Macintosh but on other computers as well. The PC/AT is particularly well supported, with a good version of PageMaker as well as Ventura Publisher and other page make-up software. The IBM PS/2 micros are able to run this PC software, and with their high-resolution screens they make excellent DTP workstations, rivalling the Mac.

Figure 4.5 shows a publication I produced using my Toshiba 3100 AT-compatible running Ventura, printed on a laser printer. It is a news-sheet produced for a group holiday staying

Fig. 4.5 *News-sheet for guests arriving at a church holiday at Bideford, produced using Ventura Publisher*

Welcome to Edgehill!

The King's Church (High Wycombe & Chesham)

The holiday starts here...

Dinner tonight is at 7 pm in the dining hall of the main college building. Please be on time. The whole family is welcome at this meal.

After dinner there will be a 9 o'clock get together in the main hall. Please be there for all the latest holiday news.

Tomorrow (Sunday) has special activities and special meal times. Breakfast will be at the normal time of 8.30 am, but there will be a worship meeting afterwards (10.30 am) in the main hall. This will be followed by a cooked meal at 1 pm, and there will be tea at 6.30 pm.

A packed programme

Lots of things have been arranged for you to do at Edgehill. But remember that it's your holiday, and you are free to join in with as little or as much as you choose.

Saturday evening at 9: for the latest holiday news and information, come to this first get together.

Sunday at 3: family sports.

Sunday evening at 7.30: treasure hunt.

Monday evening at 8: video film.

Tuesday evening at 8: barn dance.

Wednesday evening: barbecue meal followed by a camp fire.

Thursday evening: mystery happening.

Friday evening: the grand finale - parties for tinies, disco for teens, and a Fairy Tale Ball for big people.

And off the campus...

What about a boat trip to Lundy? Or a fishing trip from Ilfracombe? Or visit Dartington Glass Factory? Or go on a nature reserve ramble? Or shop at Bideford market (Wed)?

Rules of the house

1 Wash up any cups, spoons, etc that you use for drinks in your house kitchen ... otherwise your house parents will go bananas.

2 Be in by locking-up time (11 pm), unless you have obtained a key from your house parents ... otherwise they will go completely bananas.

3 Don't smoke in any of the buildings ... your house parents will disapprove. They might also get charred in the ensuing fire.

4 Don't take glass utensils to the pool, as they might break. Your house parents' bottoms will then get scarred.

5 Wear trainers or plimsolls in the gym ... other footwear will damage the floor and bring forth cries of anguish from your house parents.

6 Be jolly glad you're not a house parent.

The people who won't be glad this week are:

Carrisbrooke - Roger & Jackie King and Dave & Jackie Townsend

Belvoir - Dave & Pauline Jagger

Longfield - Simon & Linda Crisp

Remember...
Water can kill! Don't bathe alone in the pool, and don't let your child use the pool unless an adult is present.

The gastronomic agenda

Meals will be in the dining hall. Please be punctual ... a telephone bell will be rung in your house 5-10 minutes before meals.

Breakfast: 8.30 am

Dinner: 6.45 pm, except on Saturday and Sunday

Collect packed lunches after breakfast. Don't forget your lunchboxes!

If you are under 5...

... you will have your own special meal at 5.30 pm. But please ask either your mummy or your daddy to come with you. They won't pinch any of your food, as they will have their meal at 6.45 pm. You won't be able to pinch any of their food either, as you will be in the creche at that time.

Things to do at Edgehill

Swimming: the pool is open 7 am till late evening.

Reading: the book shop is open for half-an-hour each day after breakfast.

Writing: the book shop sells stamps for all those postcards.

Eating: the book shop doubles as a tuck shop. In fact, there is more tuck than books.

Exercising: Mim will be holding her keep-fit sessions at 10 am.

Playing: table tennis etc in the gym, or tennis on the tennis courts.

Washing: if you have young children you can use the laundry, but please combine loads. Roger will be there after breakfast for half-an-hour on Tuesday and Friday to assist.

Praying: there will be a prayer meeting in Longfield House at 7.45 am.

at Edgehill College, Bideford. As with virtually all DTP publications, it was produced on A4 paper (which is the size used by
desktop laser printers). Figure 4.6 shows another example of
what's possible with DTP, taken from the publication *Inside IT*.

Fig. 4.6   *Page from* Inside IT *(24 May 1987), produced using a DTP
package*

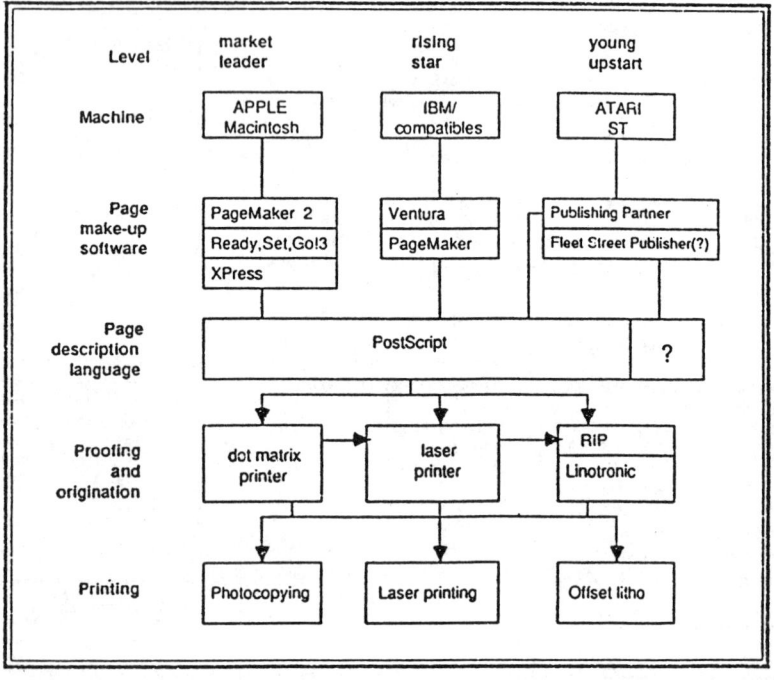

4.6   Creating a Publication

Desktop publishing packages such as PageMaker and Ventura
are designed for 'making up' pages. This is an electronic scissors-
and-glue operation involving the positioning of blocks of text
and graphics on the page and applying appropriate effects such
as different styles and sizes of type.

DTP packages are not, however, intended for originating the
text and graphics – for this you need word processing software
and painting and drawing software. DTP packages are, though,

becoming more powerful, and they incorporate some WP and drawing facilities, allowing you to do a certain amount of text editing and to create simple graphics.

The procedure for creating a publication is first to create your text and graphics using WP and graphics software, saving your work as files on disk, and then to *import* (i.e. read) these files into your DTP software. DTP packages are able to read text files created on a variety of word processing packages, as well as standard ASCII text, and they can read picture files created on most drawing and painting packages.

When you run a DTP package, it is in fact quite a simple task to read in these files and position the material they contain on the page. All DTP software contains a number of aids to assist in this positioning task, including the facility to zoom up on (i.e. magnify) a part of the page to increase the accuracy of your work, and *gridlock* or *guideline* features to line up material accurately against an invisible grid of points or a guideline.

With some DTP packages, a page consists of one or more *frames*. These are boxes that you mark out on the screen, into which you insert your files of text or graphics. One frame can hold only one file. Frames can be easily moved around the page, resized, and the material within them can be replaced with other material. Ventura is an example of this type of software, and page makeup in this case involves deciding what frames you need on your page, marking them out, and then importing the appropriate files into each.

Note that the edges of frames are invisible when printed out, though you can if you wish create a border around a frame consisting of one or more lines of whatever thickness you choose.

Many DTP packages, of which Ventura is a notable example, also provide *style sheets*. These apply a ready-made style to your publication. This will consist of preset styles and sizes for headlines, body text, etc. as well as columns and other effects. You merely have to select a suitable style sheet from the many on offer, load it, and the basic design task is done!

Because style sheets are set up by experts, they allow people with little talent for design to create good-looking publications very quickly. (The design of the publication shown on page 63 was produced by applying a ready-made style sheet provided with the Ventura DTP package.) And if you do have design talents and wish to modify a style sheet to suit your publication or your personal preferences, it is easy to do so.

The steps involved in creating a publication on a DTP package are as follows:

1 Plan the design out in rough by sketching it on a piece of paper. The design will be affected by the number of pages that you intend for the publication, and whether it will be single-sided or double-sided. Normally, your DTP system will produce A4 documents, and so you should plan for this. You will also have to decide the number of columns you will use and their width, the size and position of titles, where the headers (if any) and the page numbers are to go, and so on. In the case of frame-based packages, you should mark on your design the positions of the frames you will be using to hold your material.

2 If your DTP package provides style sheets, select the one that most nearly matches your requirements.

3 Create the text for your publication using a word processing package. In the case of a publication with a number of sections (such as that shown on page 63), each section should normally be a separate WP file, one file for each frame that you will be setting up on your DTP page.

4 Create any graphics, using, if necessary, a graphics package or scanner. In the case of very simple graphics, the DTP package's own graphics facilities may suffice. If you want to incorporate a photograph, say, in your publication, you can capture it onto disk using a scanner and associated software.

5 Set up the framework of your publication in the DTP package. In the case of packages which utilise style sheets and frames, such as Ventura Publisher, this means firstly loading the appropriate style sheet, and secondly creating the frames into which you will import your text and graphics.

6 Import your text and graphics into the appropriate frames, and carry out any adjustments required so that they fit onto the page to produce a good-looking result. For example, you may have to shorten or lengthen a section of text to fit the frame, by deleting or adding words, or you may need to adjust the amount of white space between sections or paragraphs. You could adjust frame sizes and positions. You might even need to adjust the character size and style of a section of text, though this should be done with care, as too many different sizes and styles within a publication can look untidy.

7 Print a copy of your publication and check its appearance on paper. Also check it for any errors, e.g. in spelling or style of writing. Make your final changes, then print a finished master copy, ready for the offset litho or photocopier.

You can see that desktop publishing can be quite a time-consuming job – and this is quite apart from the time that it takes to produce the original text on a word processor. Although the finished result is excellent, it is not cost-effective to use it for ordinary office typing jobs such as producing letters.

4.7 Formatting Your Text

A major feature of DTP packages is their ability to apply a huge range of character styles and sizes to your text. Used with laser printers, they provide the kind of sophisticated text formatting that traditionally could only be achieved by professional typesetters, such as those outlined below.

- Kerning, i.e. adjusting the spacing between characters to take account of their shape. To see what I mean, look at the position of the letter 'o' at the start of this sentence – its left edge is below the arm of the 'T'. This contrasts with ordinary typing (or computer printing), which leaves an unsightly gap between the vertical stem of the 'T' and the 'o'.
- Leading, pronounced 'ledding', i.e. adjusting the spacing between lines. This term originated with the practice of inserting strips of lead between the lines of type in traditional printing.
- Fonts, i.e. different styles and sizes of type. These have names inherited from traditional printing, such as the popular 'Times Roman' and 'Helvetica'. Besides the ability to embolden or italicise a font, DTP packages allow you to apply a wide range of sizes to it. These sizes are measured in 'points'. A normal size for the main body of material in your publication (called body text) is between 8 point and 12 point. Note that 1 point = $1/72$ inch.

Assignment 2

This assignment can be done either using a word processing package alone, or, if you have the time and suitable software, using a DTP package as well.

Design and draft an A4-sized advert describing some of the features of a word processing package that you are able to use in your college. You should begin by spending some time practising with the package in order to master its main facilities, and you should make notes on those facilities which you think should feature in your advert. To get an idea of what's wanted, glance through some adverts for WP or other software in computer magazines. One advert is shown in Figure 4.1 on page 51.

Then create the text of your advert using the word processing package. Take advantage of features like emboldening to enhance its appearance. If possible, make use of a DTP package to make up and print your advert in the most attractive and eye-catching way. Hand the finished result to your tutor for marking.

Questions

1 Word processing offers numerous advantages over ordinary typing, many of which have been outlined in this chapter. Besides these, WP offers special benefits for certain types of business. Give ONE special advantage for each of the following. The answer to the first is given on page 55.
   a A solicitor.
   b An estate agent.
   c A student writing to a number of employers for jobs.

2 It is estimated that word processing doubles productivity in many typing situations, and it gives a higher-quality result. Give three reasons for the productivity improvements, and three for the quality improvements.

3 A school office has a personal computer with both word processing and desktop publishing. Give two jobs that it will do using the WP package, and two that it will do using the DTP package.

4 Think of three applications of outlining software that would help you with your college work.

5 Before the advent of desktop publishing, businesses sent publishing work such as brochures out to professional type-setters and printers. Now they can produce these publications in-house. Think of three advantages and two disadvantages of producing your own publications using DTP.

6 Why might a paragraph of ordinary text look better printed from a DTP package than from a WP package?

Chapter 5
Record Keeping and Spreadsheets

This chapter looks at how computers can be used to keep records and manage tables of data. Examples of the former include personnel records, stock records, and student records. Examples of the latter include things like tables of monthly sales of a firm (to produce totals, averages, etc.) and, on a bleaker note, tables of students' exam results.

In the jargon of the computer world, a file of records is called a *database*, and a table or 'sheet' of data is called a *worksheet*. Record-keeping software is called *database management* software, and software for handling a worksheet is called a *spreadsheet*.

There are some similarities between records and worksheets, and some jobs can be done using either a database package or a spreadsheet. One example is student records – you can either create one 'record card' for each student, with his or her address and all assignment and exam results on that card, or you can put that data onto one row of a worksheet. In the former case, data for the whole class is held in a file of record cards, in the latter it is held as successive rows of a worksheet.

There are, however, important differences. Database software allows you to rapidly retrieve selected records (such as all those with over 70% in their IT exam), to sort records into sequence, and to do jobs like automatically producing end-of-year letters to students with their results.

Spreadsheet software, in contrast, enables you to do much more in the way of calculations on the rows and columns of the worksheet. It also provides facilities for producing charts and graphs of your data.

Which type of software you use depends on what you want to do with the data. This chapter covers the main features of both, and describes some typical applications.

5.1 Database Concepts

In the context of record-keeping systems, a database is simply a file of records, not dissimilar to a card index system. In its broadest sense, however, a database is any collection of data, not necessarily organised into electronic record cards. It includes, for example, the data held in the Bible or on Prestel. You will meet some of these other types of databases in Chapter 6.

Sticking with the card index idea, there are a number of database concepts that you need to know. The most obvious one is *record*, which refers to the data held on one individual or entity: a student, in the case of a student record system, or an item of stock in the case of a stock record system. In manual systems, such as a card index, a record may be called a 'card'; in the case of computer systems, however, it is more usual to refer to it as a *form*.

In a card index, each card has printed on it a number of headings or *labels*. In the case of an index of names and addresses, for example, the labels might be:

forename
surname
street
town

and so on. To the right of each label there is a space or *field* to hold the data or *values*. Each card in the index has an identical design of labels and fields printed on it, but the data held on each will be different. The index of identically-printed cards is called a *file*.

The same is true in a computerised record-keeping system. Each form in a file will have an identical design, consisting of fields and field labels.

Just as there are card indexes for many different kinds of records, such as patients' details in a hospital, or stock held in a warehouse, so a computer database package can be used for many different jobs. Each job will be stored on a different file with a different form design.

For example, here are two of the tasks for which I use a database package on my computer.

- To keep records of my income and outgoings in connection with writing books. One advantage of using the computer for this is that it produces automatically the financial statement required by the taxman at the end of the year.
- To keep records of people coming on a holiday at Bideford that I helped to organise. (You glanced at the news-sheet for this on page 63.)

A record from the first 'accounts' file is shown in Figure 5.1, with the field labels at the left and the data on the right. I shall be referring to this file later on, so it's worth pointing out here that I have chosen the label 'Type' to refer to the type of transaction – normally a receipt or an expense. 'Category' refers to the receipt or expense category in which the transaction lies – in the case of an expense, it might be 'Hardware' (that I buy), 'Software', 'Prestel fees', 'Consumables' (e.g. paper for my printer), and so on.

A record from the second 'holiday' file is shown in Figure 5.2. Note in this example that the computer calculates all of the money figures automatically, as well as the totals. Note too that the database software that I use (Q&A) enables me to do things like drawing a box round the form to enhance its appearance.

Fig. 5.1 *A form from my accounts file*

```
                 PERSONAL    ACCOUNTS

           Type: Capital expense

       Category: Software

    Description: Powermenu

           Date: 11/5/88

         Amount: £62.00
```

Fig. 5.2 *A form from the holiday file*

```
                          BIDEFORD HOLIDAY 1988

Surname: O'Connor                     Forename: Mick
Church: Wycombe                       Phone:

Numbers booked -                      Costs -
                     Adults: 2                  £130.00
                    12 - 16: 0                    £0.00
                     7 - 11: 1                   £35.00
                      3 - 6: 1                   £30.00
                      0 - 2: 1
                (Under 12s: 3 )
                     TOTAL: 5                   £195.00

Deposit received:  £30.00             Acknowledgement printed? Y
     Balance due: £165.00

Balance received? Y                   Acknowledgement printed? Y
```

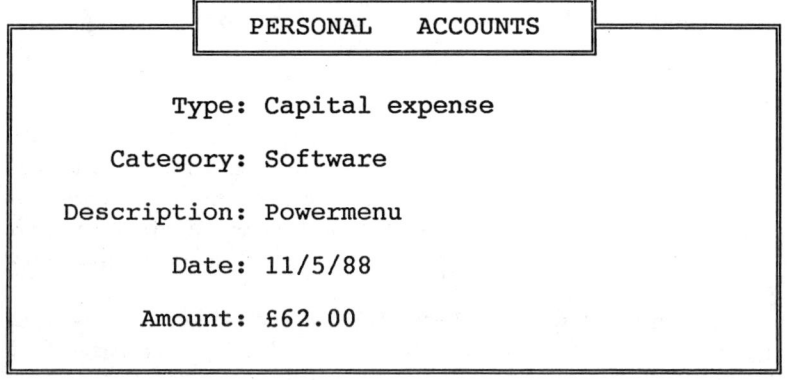

5.2 Using a Database Package

Database management packages vary widely in the way that they work. Some, like dBase, are command-driven (see Chapter 3). You will probably work with a package that is menu-driven (or else with dBase in its menu-driven mode). The facilities offered also differ from package to package, and each package will approach the record-keeping task in its own way. However, the kinds of things that you can do, and the order in which you do them, are the same whichever package you use, and they are described in this section.

a) Design the form
If you want to set up a record-keeping system, the first task is to design the form. This means specifying the field labels and the size of each field. Many modern database packages operate rather like word processors at the form design stage, allowing you to type your field labels at the required position on the screen and then to mark out the fields in some way. Many also allow you to embellish your design with headings and boxes, like the forms shown in Figures 5.1 and 5.2.

As part of the form design phase you normally have to specify whether the data (i.e. values) that are to be entered into a field are to be text, numbers, money, dates, or some other category. This is to enable the software to format your data properly. If you specify 'money', for example, the software will display it in the format of the currency of your choice.

When you start using a database you have designed, you will think of improvements that you can make. With modern database packages it is easy to make alterations to the design, such as changing field labels or moving them around the form, adding fields, and deleting fields. You can make these changes even after you have started adding records to your database.

The design of your form, together with any reports that might be attached to it (see below), is called a *template*. Often, when designing a new system, you can use the template from an existing system, making relatively simple adjustments to tailor it to your new requirements. This can save a great deal of time. For some of the more popular packages, such as dBase, these templates can be purchased commercially.

b) Enter data
Your database is no use until you have typed some data into it, i.e. entered values to create records. In the case of my 'accounts' file, for example, each time I receive a royalty payment for a book

or incur an item of expenditure, I use Q&A to retrieve my accounts file and add to it a record for that transaction. So over the course of a year, this file grows from nothing to many dozens of records, each one representing a transaction.

Once the data is entered, most database packages automatically save it to disk.

c) Retrieve records

If you wish to look at, update, or delete a record or group of records, you must retrieve it from the file so that it is displayed on your computer screen. Database software offers you a variety of retrieval options. For example, you can retrieve all records that match a value in a certain field, or several values in several fields, or a few characters from a value.

Suppose, for example, I want to see all records of items of expenditure in my accounts file. I select Q&A's 'Search/Update' menu option, and then type 'Expense' in the 'Type' field as the entry to be matched. Q&A then searches the file for the records that match this and presents them, one at a time, on the screen.

The records can also be sorted into order before being presented on the screen. This might be in ascending order of date, or ascending order of category, or whatever other sort order I choose.

d) Print data

As well as being viewed on the screen, forms can also be printed out. Besides this, selected values from the forms can be printed as a list, each selected field corresponding to a column on the page.

It is also possible to merge data from selected records with a document prepared on a word processor, to carry out the kind of 'mailmerge' job described in the last chapter. In the case of the word processing module of Q&A, for example, all that is needed is to insert the field labels within asterisks in the appropriate places in the document. On printing, these will be replaced by the values from those fields. Document after document will be printed, as data from each record is merged with the standard text.

e) Produce reports

A 'report', in the context of a database, means summaries of the data. This includes totals, averages, and other measures which give the key facts about the database. In the case of my accounts, for example, the key facts include the total receipts and the total expenses, and the difference between the two. A report will also normally include data from selected fields listed in columns.

Figure 5.3 is an example of a report, produced from an accounts file similar to the one described earlier, summarising the income and expenditure transactions for the Bideford holiday. Note the following points:

- the transactions have been retrieved from the database and listed in order: first, in descending order of transaction type (receipt or expense); second, in ascending order of 'description'; third, in ascending order of date;
- totals and subtotals have been calculated and inserted at appropriate points.

This particular report provides all the information needed, in the right form, for an auditor or anyone else wishing to examine the state of the holiday accounts.

It is a quick and easy job to design a report such as this in a package like Q&A. You merely have to specify the fields that are to appear as columns in the report, whether the data in those fields are to be listed in order, and which columns require calculations (totals, subtotals, averages, etc.). Once the report is designed, it can be run (i.e. printed) at any time, retrieving data from the database and calculating totals and other results quite automatically.

f) Maintain your database
Besides the above tasks, there are some routine jobs that you need to do with your database. One is to remove records which are no longer current, and to update those whose details have changed. In the case of a file of customer names and addresses, for example, you should remove records of customers who no longer deal with you, and amend the records of any who have moved to new addresses.

Another maintenance task is making periodic backups of your files. These should be stored on floppy disks away from the computer in case of accident. Many businesses make daily backups, so important is their data to their survival.

Some files are used to store data relating to just one year (or other time period). At the end of that period you then have to start a new file, using the template from the original. My accounts file is an example of this – next April I will start again with the accounts for the new financial year. In this situation the old file should be safely stored on floppy disk (or archived in some other way), and the new file brought into being.

With computers, it is important that this kind of housekeeping

Fig. 5.3 *Report produced from the Bideford holiday accounts file*

```
HOLIDAY ACCOUNTS AT 1 September 1988
```

Rec/Exp	Category	Description	Date	Amount
Receipt	Bankings	From bookings	19/03/88	£260.00
		From bookings	09/04/88	£280.00
		From bookings	26/04/88	£190.00
		From bookings	03/05/88	£60.00
		From bookings	12/05/88	£120.00
		From bookings	01/06/88	£350.00
		From bookings	14/06/88	£290.00
		From bookings	23/06/88	£575.00
		From bookings	28/06/88	£3005.00
		From bookings	06/07/88	£1245.00
		From bookings	28/07/88	£385.00
		From bookings	01/08/88	£380.00
		From bookings	04/08/88	£140.00
		From Petty Cash	08/08/88	£62.72
		From petty cash	15/08/88	£127.34
		Interest	08/08/88	£5.47
	Total:			£7475.53
	Cash	From bookings	28/06/88	£100.00
		From bookings	03/07/88	£240.00
		From bookings	08/07/88	£110.00
		From bookings	11/07/88	£50.00
		From bookings	28/07/88	£155.00
		From bookings	30/07/88	£40.00
		From bookings	03/08/88	£25.00
	Total:			£720.00
Total:				£8195.53
Expense	Accommodation	Edgehill College	03/08/88	£3275.72
	Total:			£3275.72
	Decorations	Hire of costumes	21/07/88	£69.00
	Total:			£69.00
	Food	Booker-Steed	28/07/88	£172.92
		Children's party	04/08/88	£23.15
		Express Dairy Ltd	08/08/88	£174.20
		Express Dairy Ltd	14/08/88	£189.13
		Farm Fresh Butchers	29/07/88	£224.58
		Farm Fresh Butchers	02/08/88	£10.93
		Farm Fresh Butchers	02/08/88	£79.37
		Farm Fresh Butchers	03/08/88	£169.22
		Farm Fresh Butchers	05/08/88	£6.91
		Farm Fresh Butchers	05/08/88	£9.00
		G.H.Little (Vegetables)	29/07/88	£24.42
		G.H.Little (Vegetables)	01/08/88	£44.11
		G.H.Little (Vegetables)	02/08/88	£4.00
		G.H.Little (Vegetables)	02/08/88	£52.71
		G.H.Little (Vegetables)	03/08/88	£32.65
		G.H.Little (Vegetables)	05/08/88	£53.05
		Scott's Model Bakery	01/08/88	£49.05
		Scott's Model Bakery	02/08/88	£25.65
		Scott's Model Bakery	03/08/88	£44.85
		Scott's Model Bakery	05/08/88	£49.05
		Scott's Model Bakery	05/08/88	£25.65
	Total:			£1464.60
	Petty cash	Cash held back from bookings	28/06/88	£100.00
		Cash held back from bookings	03/07/88	£240.00
		Cash held back from bookings	08/07/88	£110.00
		Cash held back from bookings	11/07/88	£50.00
		Cash held back from bookings	28/07/88	£155.00
		Cash held back from bookings	30/07/88	£40.00
		Cash held back from bookings	03/08/88	£25.00
		Withdrawn from bank	16/06/88	£100.00
		Withdrawn from bank	28/07/88	£500.00
		Withdrawn from bank	01/08/88	£1000.00
		Withdrawn from bank	04/08/88	£1000.00
	Total:			£3320.00
	Sundries	Hire of video films	15/08/88	£18.00
	Total:			£18.00
Total:				£8147.32

task is carried out systematically and conscientiously, otherwise your files can become cluttered up with unwanted records, or you can lose valuable data. To make life easy for you, database packages always provide menu options for making backups of files, deleting records, and other housekeeping tasks.

5.3 Other Features of Database Packages

Besides these tasks that all database packages can be expected to support, most database packages will also have features like the following:

- *data validation facilities*, meaning that the software will check that any values that you enter are valid (i.e. 'acceptable'). This facility will automatically check that any value typed in is of the right type (e.g. a date, a number, or whatever is the field type), and, if a number, that it is within the acceptable range, if one has been specified. For example, in a student database that records grades and exam marks, you would want the database to reject a mark lying outside the range 0 – 100, as this would clearly be an error;

- *large file size*. Most database packages do not load the whole file of records into RAM but work with it on disk, loading merely the currently-retrieved record or group of records. The file size is therefore limited by the disk capacity rather than the space available in RAM, so these packages will allow you to store many thousands of records in a single file. The drawback of this is that it can take a relatively long time – perhaps as much as two or three minutes – to search through a large file containing thousands of records, compared to the almost instant response if they are all held in RAM. (Spreadsheet packages, in contrast, normally hold all their data in RAM, speeding up operations but limiting the worksheet size.);

- *automatic calculations in results fields*. An example of this can be seen in Figure 5.2 (the holiday bookings form), where total numbers coming on the holiday, the amounts due, and so on, are automatically worked out by the computer and inserted in the appropriate fields. Q&A, the package used to set up this file, allows you to enter formulae which perform these calculations in selected fields, a feature which resembles the calculating facility provided in spreadsheet packages described later. Once entered, these formulae sit invisibly in the background – which is why you can't see them in Figures 5.1 and 5.2.

5.4   Cardbox and Relational Databases

I've likened a database to a box of index cards, and for most easy-to-use packages such as Q&A this is a valid comparison. In fact, these packages are sometimes called *cardbox* packages because of this likeness. By their nature, these packages are only able to work with one file at a time.

More complex packages are able to work with several files at the same time, relating entries in one to entries in another. These are called *relational* database packages.

To help you understand the difference between these two types of package, suppose you work on the computer in the sales department of a firm. You have two main files that you work with, namely:

- the customer file, which has one record per customer with his or her name and address, and onto which you enter details of all orders received from customers – the products purchased, the price, the date of purchase, and so on;

- the product file, which has one record per product line, holding details such as the price, quantities received from suppliers and dates, quantities issued to customers and dates, the balance in stock, and so on.

You can imagine that your job would be made very efficient if, when you key into the customer file the code number of a product purchased, the computer automatically extracts the product's name, the price and other details from the product file and inserts them in the customer's record; and at the same time updates the product file with numbers of the product that have been issued. That is exactly what a relational database does – it automatically links files together, updating one with information from another.

Often, more than two files will be linked in this way. In the above sales situation, for instance, there will normally be three files:

- an order file containing details of the order (the customer's code number, the product code numbers and quantities, and the date), from which the total order value is calculated and invoices and delivery notes produced;

- a customer file containing the customer's name and address, the values of orders and the dates, from which the monthly statement is produced;

- a product file containing the product details such as quantities received and issued, and from which purchase orders are produced to send to suppliers.

The order file picks up the customer details from the customer file, and the product details from the product file. It in turn updates the customer file with the value of the order, and the product file with the number of issues. This is illustrated in Figure 5.4.

Fig. 5.4 *Example of linked files in a relational database*

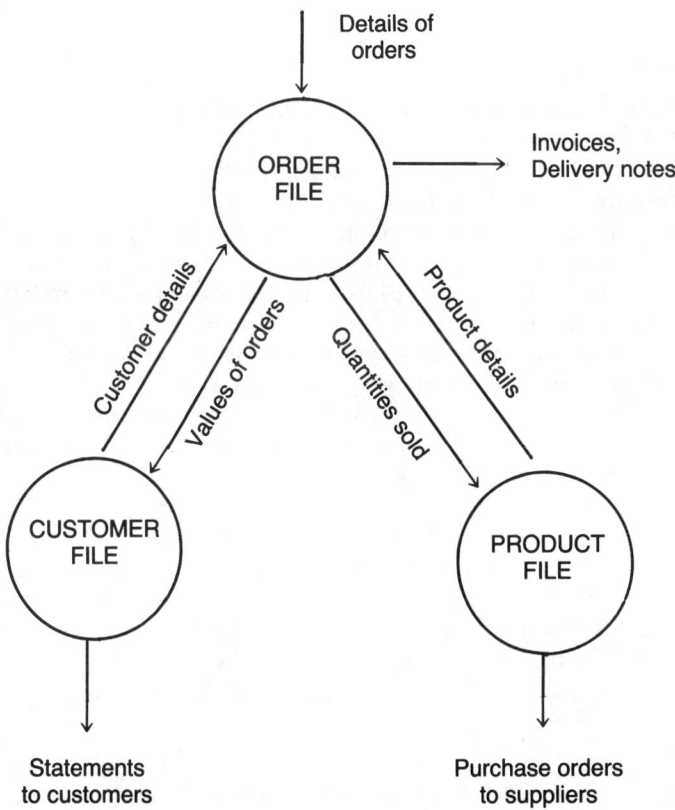

This is a greatly simplified account of what actually goes on in a sales accounting situation, but it illustrates the value of relational databases.

Relational database packages are clearly much more powerful and useful than cardbox packages. They are, however, more expensive to purchase, and more difficult to learn and use. Most office record-keeping tasks are 'cardbox' tasks, and for these it makes sense to use a simpler cardbox package. With these simpler packages you can design and set up systems very quickly, and they are quick and easy to use when you want to access the data or produce reports.

The most well-known relational database is dBase III, recently replaced by an improved version called dBase IV. A number of other similar packages are also available, many of which claim to offer more features at a lower price. Typical prices for relational database packages are £500 or more, whereas cardbox packages generally cost around £200 or less.

5.5 Spreadsheets

Instead of storing data as records in a file, spreadsheet packages store data as rows in a table or 'worksheet'. Each column will normally be labelled with a heading in the top row, and these correspond to the field labels in a record.

An example of a worksheet is shown in Figure 5.5. This calculates the monthly cash flows of a business from its receipts and expenses. The column labels in this case are the months of the year. The items that make up the cash in (i.e. the receipts) and the cash out (i.e. the expenses) are the row headings listed down the left. In certain respects each row corresponds to a record in a database, though this comparison can be a little misleading. The calculated rows at the bottom of the worksheet, for example, do not correspond to records.

(In case you are not familiar with the idea of calculating cash flows, the 'monthly cash position' in this worksheet gives the difference between the cash received (i.e. total income) and the cash paid out (total expenditure). This is added to the amount of cash carried forward ('working capital') from the previous month to arrive at the new working capital position. Study the values in the bottom rows of Figure 5.5 to confirm for yourself that they are calculated in this way.)

Fig. 5.5 *Worksheet for calculating cash flows*

	A	B	C	D	E	F
1		SEP	OCT	NOV	DEC	JAN
2		-------	-------	-------	-------	-------
3	CASH FLOW IN					
4	Sales (Debtors)	3450.00	15410.00	24208.00	27428.00	24815.00
5	Bank loans		30000.00			
6	Directors' input	10000.00				
7	Other					
8		-------	-------	-------	-------	-------
9	Total Income	13450.00	45410.00	24208.00	27428.00	24815.00
10	==
11	CASH FLOW OUT					
12	Purchases	8750.00	7060.00	8440.00	5450.00	6670.00
13	Wages	4020.00	4225.00	4225.00	4225.00	4225.00
14	Rent and rates	450.00	450.00	450.00	450.00	450.00
15	Electricity		1125.00			
16	Insurances	410.00	410.00	410.00	410.00	410.00
17	Telephone			919.00		
18	Postage & stationery	450.00	450.00	450.00	450.00	450.00
19	Advertizing	3509.00	3509.00	3509.00	3509.00	3509.00
20	Exhibition expenses	1533.00	1533.00	1533.00	1533.00	1533.00
21	Travelling expenses	958.00	958.00	958.00	958.00	958.00
22	Legal & professional		2323.00			
23	Sundries	392.00	355.00	412.00	460.00	354.00
24	Bank charges	150.00			200.00	
25	Bank interest				900.00	
26	Loan repayments			2000.00	2000.00	2000.00
27	HP payments	409.00	409.00	409.00	409.00	409.00
28		-------	-------	-------	-------	-------
29	Total expenditure	21031.00	22807.00	23715.00	20954.00	20968.00
30	==
31	MONTHLY CASH POSITION	-7581.00	22603.00	493.00	6474.00	3847.00
32	WORKING CAPITAL	-7581.00	15022.00	15515.00	21989.00	25836.00
33	==

One of the most common uses of spreadsheets is to produce cash-flow forecasts, so that businesses can make better plans. The procedure is to enter the expected receipts and expenses for the months ahead, and the formulae stored in the worksheet will automatically and instantly calculate the expected cash position. You can then investigate what happens if, say, you increase wages by 5%. Simply enter the new figures in the wages row, and the computer immediately calculates the new cash position.

This is called a 'What if' investigation, and it is one of the greatest benefits of spreadsheets. Managers and other decision-makers can quickly assess the outcomes of certain courses of action, without actually carrying them out. If poor results are indicated, then a different course of action can be tried out on the worksheet.

Worksheets that are set up to do this kind of thing are called 'models', because they are computer representations of some aspect of real life. In the case of a cash-flow forecast, the worksheet is modelling the income and expenditure of the business.

Of course, models are never 100% accurate, which means that the results that they forecast will not exactly match what would actually happen. This is not the fault of the computer, of course, but arises from the fact that no model can take account of the myriad possibilities that can arise. In the case of the cash-flow forecast, any values entered for future sales and purchases are only estimates, and are bound to differ somewhat from the actual sales and purchases that the business achieves.

Although somewhat inaccurate, forecasts such as these are very much better than no forecasts at all, and they have been of immense benefit to business. It was, in fact, the development of spreadsheet software able to carry out this kind of analysis that led to businesses first becoming interested in microcomputers back in the late 1970s. Packages that aid decision-making in this way are called *decision-support* software.

Spreadsheets are not only used for decision-support, however, and there are a large number of purely clerical applications. One example is the kind of accounting application described in the database section of this chapter. Some businesses keep their accounts on a spreadsheet, with column labels representing the type of receipt or expense, and each transaction representing one row.

If I kept my personal accounts in this way instead of using a database package, my column labels would include 'Royalties', 'Prestel fees', 'Software costs', 'Repairs', and so on. In the case of the business used in the cash-flow example in Figure 5.5, the column labels would be the list of items on the left (Sales, Bank Loans, etc.).

Besides these financial applications, spreadsheets are widely used in many other fields, including engineering, archaeology, and zoology, to mention just a few. Of more relevance to commerce students are applications like manpower planning, budgeting, investment analysis, and the like, all of which are now carried out using spreadsheets.

5.6 Spreadsheets and Databases Compared

From what I've said, you have probably realised that one of the main objects of spreadsheets is to carry out calculations of one sort and another on rows and columns of figures. They are very good at this, offering more in the way of calculating features than do database packages. Because of this, spreadsheets are used with data that is mainly numerical, rather than for things like names and addresses. Database packages, in contrast, are good at retrieving data, searching, and sorting, and they are used with files containing both text and data values.

One of the values of integrated packages is that they allow you to handle the same file of data in both the database module and in the spreadsheet module, giving you the best of both worlds. Other software, though, offers similar facilities: Q&A, for instance, has links with the Lotus 1-2-3 spreadsheet package, allowing you to switch files easily between them.

5.7 Spreadsheet Concepts

An important spreadsheet concept is the *cell*, which is the space lying at the intersection of a row and a column, into which data is typed. Each value in the worksheet in Figure 5.5, for example, is located in its own cell. A worksheet therefore consists of a grid or matrix of cells, and, like points on a map, these cells are identified by their horizontal and vertical co-ordinates.

The horizontal co-ordinates are letters assigned in sequence to each column, starting with 'A' for the left-most column and continuing through the alphabet to Z and then through further columns labelled AA, AB, AC, and so on. The vertical co-ordinates are numbers assigned in sequence to each row, starting at '1' for the top row.

Figure 5.6 illustrates this. It shows the top left hand corner of a simple worksheet, with the columns lettered and the rows numbered. The word 'EGGS' is located in cell A1, and the value '3.00' is in B2. Note that these column letters and row numbers appear on the screen, but they are not printed when you produce a hardcopy of your worksheet.

Fig. 5.6 *Simple worksheet for calculating a shopping list*

	A	B	C
1	EGGS	2.00	
2	BACON	3.00	
3	HAM	4.00	
4	TOTAL	9.00	

Spreadsheet packages allow you to create worksheets with hundreds of columns and thousands of rows, the exact number you can get being determined in practice by the amount of RAM that is available in your computer and the amount of data stored in the worksheet. As I said earlier, the whole of the worksheet is held in RAM.

You will be familiar with many of the other concepts used in spreadsheet work from what you've read in this book about word processing and record keeping. Familiar concepts include the following:

- *cursor* – the point at which your next typed entry will appear is shown by a highlighted cursor on the screen, in this case occupying an entire cell;
- *scroll* – a worksheet will not normally fit within the confines of the computer screen, and so to see other parts you have to scroll through it by moving the cursor. As with word processing, the arrow keys (or the mouse) are used for this, larger jumps being possible using e.g. CTRL and the arrow keys, or the Home, End, PgUp, and PgDn keys. The use of some of these keys and key combinations may vary slightly from package to package;
- *formula* – a cell entry, normally residing invisibly in the background, which calculates the value to be displayed in that cell. The calculation is based on the contents of other cells, and so a formula consists of cell references. For example, in Figure 5.6 the formula B1+B2+B3 contained in cell B4 tells the computer: 'Add the value in B1 and the value in B2 and the value in B3 and place the result in B5'. If the price of one of the commodities is altered, say £2.00 for the price of eggs is changed to £3.00, then the formula instantly changes the total, in this case from £9 to £10.

5.8 Spreadsheet Operations

Unlike database packages, spreadsheet packages differ little from each other in their ways of working. One reason for this is that most of them are based on the original 'Visicalc' spreadsheet developed in the 70s. Here's a list of the basic operations you perform with these spreadsheets to enter data and formulae and to access the menu system.

(Note that in WIMP environments, such as the Mac environment, you will normally use the mouse to move the cursor around and to access the menu, rather than the keyboard operations described below. Note also that a few spreadsheet packages do not fit into the Visicalc tradition, and so some of what's said here will not apply to these. Microsoft's Multiplan is an example of a non-standard spreadsheet.)

- When you run the spreadsheet, a blank worksheet (table) appears on the screen, with the columns lettered and the rows numbered. You can move the cursor around using the arrow keys and the other keys indicated earlier.

- To enter a value in a cell, first move the cursor to that cell, then type the value, then press the ENTER key. As you type the value it will appear at the top left or bottom left of the screen (depending on the package), but will be transferred to the cell as soon as you press ENTER. The cursor will still be located on that cell, so to move it to an adjacent cell you will have to press an arrow key. To save some time, you can press the arrow key instead of ENTER after typing the value, and the computer will place the value in the cell and move you to the adjacent cell in a single operation.

- The spreadsheet will line up text entries at the left edge of the cell, but numerical values will be aligned from the right. Figure 5.5 illustrates this. In most cases, this is fine, but there are occasions when you want text entries to be right-aligned, or centred. The names of the months at the top of the columns of Figure 5.5 are an example – they are best aligned to the right or centred, so that they are immediately above the numerical values to which they refer. To right-align a text entry, you normally precede it with the " symbol, and to centre it you should precede it with a ^.

- To tell the computer to left-align a number, precede it by the symbol " – though note that this will make the computer regard this value as text. Telephone numbers, for example, should be converted to text in this way, otherwise strange things can happen – the initial 0 might be omitted from the dialling code, or the number might be displayed to two decimal places.

- To enter a formula, you must tell the computer that it is not a value for displaying in the cell. To do this, you must precede it with a mathematical symbol, typically a '+'. So the formula on the previous page (for Figure 5.6) should be entered as +B1+B2+B3.

- To access the menu system, press the / symbol. The main menu options will then be displayed across the top or bottom of the screen. To select an option, you press the first letter of its name. A further menu of sub-options will then appear, from which you make a selection in the same way. An alternative selection method available in many packages involves moving the cursor (or highlight bar as it has now become) along to the option with the right arrow key, then pressing ENTER to select it.

5.9   Using a Spreadsheet

The steps involved in using a spreadsheet are not unlike those for database packages. First, you must design your worksheet, then you must enter data in it, and then carry out tasks like saving, printing, and examining the results of any calculations. It is often helpful to display these results as charts or graphs, and so spreadsheets provide this kind of option also.

Let's examine these steps in detail.

a) Designing a worksheet
You will recall that the design of a database starts with deciding and typing in the field labels, and deciding the field widths and any formatting required such as the number of decimal places. Worksheet design starts in the same way. First you type in the column labels (headings), then you decide the column widths and any formatting.

It's a good idea to rough out your design on paper first, i.e. decide the column labels and possibly the row labels. If you don't get the design quite right, it's easy enough to add or delete columns later. Remember when typing in a label that you may wish to centre or right-justify it if numerical values are to go in the column, so that it lines up with the values.

Setting the column widths involves selecting the appropriate menu option and either typing in the new width (i.e. the number of characters you wish it to hold), or else altering the width on the screen using the arrow keys. The default column width – the width that the worksheet adopts automatically until you tell it otherwise – is nine characters. Setting the number of decimal places for the column is also carried out using a menu option.

An important part of the design task is entering the formulae in the cells that are to contain the results of calculations. I've already indicated briefly what's involved, but there are a number of options and possibilities, some of which are dealt with in the section on formulae below.

Once you've designed your template, you should try it out by entering a small amount of test data. Check that the formulae all work correctly, giving the same results as you obtain by using a calculator or a pencil and paper.

A large number of templates are available commercially for the more popular spreadsheet packages such as Lotus 1-2-3. These cover a wide range of financial, statistical, and other applications. You might think that it's an easy task merely to set up column labels and formulae, and that there is little to be gained in purchasing off-the-shelf templates. However, there can be much more to template design than what I've said here. You can:

- set up customized menu options for worksheets;
- set up macros to speed up the data entry task;
- create special sections of the worksheet called 'lookup tables', which enable values entered just once to be applied at many points in the worksheet;
- set up windows and borders in the worksheet, so that, for example, two related but widely separated parts of the worksheet are visible at the same time on the screen, or column labels are always visible however far down through the rows you move.

These are just some of the possibilities.

A properly designed and efficient worksheet for a complex task can take quite a time to set up and develop. Since most businesses have similar tasks that they want spreadsheets to perform, it makes sense to spread the cost of developing such templates over a large number of users by marketing them commercially. That way everyone gains.

b) Entering formulae
Spreadsheets provide a number of aids to speed up the entry of formulae. One of these is the *replicate* facility which allows you to copy a formula in one cell across a range of other cells.

Look again at the worksheet in Figure 5.5 on page 81. The formula to work out the total income for September in cell B10 is +B4+B5+B6+B7. In the case of October, the formula is +C4+C5+C6+C7. The only change is the replacement of the 'B' by the 'C' throughout the formula. Similar changes occur in the November, December, and January formulae. If you apply the spreadsheet's replicate facility to the formula in B10, copying it across the range of cells C10 to F10, the 'B' will be changed to the appropriate column letter quite automatically.

The same thing can be done with the formulae in the Total Expenditure, Monthly Cash Position, and Working Capital rows – the formulae for these need only by entered once, in the B column, and then replicated across the rest.

Another spreadsheet aid is the use of *functions* to simplify the calculating of totals, averages, and other commonly-used results.

These functions take three-character names, like SUM or AVG, preceded by the '@' symbol to tell the computer to treat them as a function and not a cell value.

Look again at Figure 5.5. Without the use of a function, the formula to work out the total expenditure in cell B29 is +B12+B13+B14+B15 and so on to +B27. This would be really tiresome to have to key in – how much simpler to use the @SUM function, which replaces this formula with @SUM(B12..B27). The two dots stand for the word 'to', which in this case says to the computer, 'use in this formula every cell in the range B12 to B27.

Naturally when you replicate this formula across the successive cells in row 29, the B's are changed to C's in the October column, D's in the November column, and so on.

c) Enter data

Once the worksheet with its formulae has been set up and tested, you can enter your data (values) into it. Whenever you type in a value which is used in formulae elsewhere in the worksheet, the spreadsheet calculates the results immediately. In the case of the worksheet in Figure 5.5, an entry in the September column will be used by the formula that works out the total for that month; it will also by used in the working capital formulae for that month and all successive months.

In the case of a very large worksheet, this automatic recalculation can take quite a few seconds and slows down the data entry task. To overcome this, you can select a menu option which turns off automatic recalculation, turning it on again when you have finished entering the data.

As with a database, you will not finish with a spreadsheet in a single session with your computer, but will come back to it repeatedly to do more work with it. So you will want to store it on disk, using the spreadsheet's 'save' option (see below), and retrieve it again later when you resume work on it.

d) Print the worksheet

Using its 'print' option, a worksheet can be printed much like a page or more of text – except that in this case the page can be very wide. Dot matrix printers provide a 'compressed' print facility allowing you to print 15 characters to the inch instead of the usual ten, and some models have wide carriages taking wide paper. Even so, you may not get all the columns on one sheet, in which case the worksheet will print what's left over on later sheets, which you can cut up afterwards and paste in the correct position.

e) Save the worksheet

As with other kinds of files, you should save your work before exiting the spreadsheet, and ideally you should save and re-save periodically during a prolonged spreadsheet session, in case of power failure, etc.

Most spreadsheets allow you to save your work not only in their own 'native' format but in other standard formats as well, for use with other software. For example, you might want to manipulate your spreadsheet as records in a database (each row becoming a record), in which case you may have to save it (i.e. *export* it) in another format.

5.10 Charts and Graphs

Unlike database packages, spreadsheets do not provide reporting facilities for summarising and analysing data. In place of this, totals and other summary measures can be designed into a worksheet, and, in addition, spreadsheets allow you to present these results in the form of charts and graphs.

Charts enable you to *compare* values in a visual way. In the cash-flow worksheet in Figure 5.5, for example, it is much easier to appreciate the growth in working capital by showing it as an ascending line on a graph rather than having to look along the row of values to compare them.

Spreadsheets vary in their charting facilities, but most allow you to produce bar charts, pie charts, and line (i.e. XY) graphs. Which chart you should use depends on the kind of data you are dealing with and the kinds of comparisons you want to make. The growth in working capital mentioned above can be clearly seen on a rising graph, but much less clearly on a pie chart. A pie chart, however, would be an excellent way of showing the share of total expenditure accounted for by each of the 'cash flow out' items.

To help you choose the most appropriate chart, here are some simple rules.

● Graphs are used to compare one set of values (plotted against the Y-axis) with another (plotted along the X-axis). They are especially useful for showing changes over time; in this case each time period – months, or years, or whatever – is plotted along the X-axis, and the amounts for each period are plotted against the Y-axis. Figure 5.7 shows a graph produced (using the Lotus 1-2-3 spreadsheet) for the cash-flow worksheet, showing the monthly growth in working capital.

- Pie charts are used to compare individual values within a set. Figure 5.8 shows a pie chart (again produced using Lotus) for the first four 'cash flow out' items for October in the cash-flow worksheet. The relative size of each slice of the pie indicates the importance of the corresponding item of expenditure relative to the rest.
- Bar charts can be used to do both of the above jobs – to compare values in a set, and to show how those values are changing with time. Figure 5.9 shows a bar chart showing total income and total expenditure over the run of months covered by the cash-flow worksheet. It shows not only the relative sizes of the total income and the total expenditure, but it indicates how they are growing over the period.

It is important to provide an explanatory title for each chart or graph that you produce, and to label the axes properly. The Figures 5.7 to 5.9 indicate what's wanted, and spreadsheet packages provide titling and labelling facilities to help with this.

Fig. 5.7   *Graph from cash-flow worksheet*

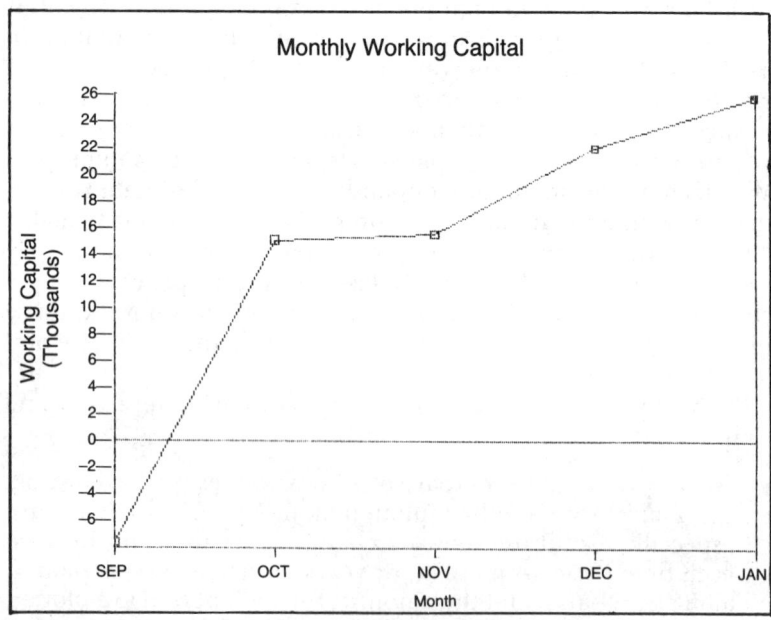

Fig. 5.8 *Pie chart from cash-flow worksheet*

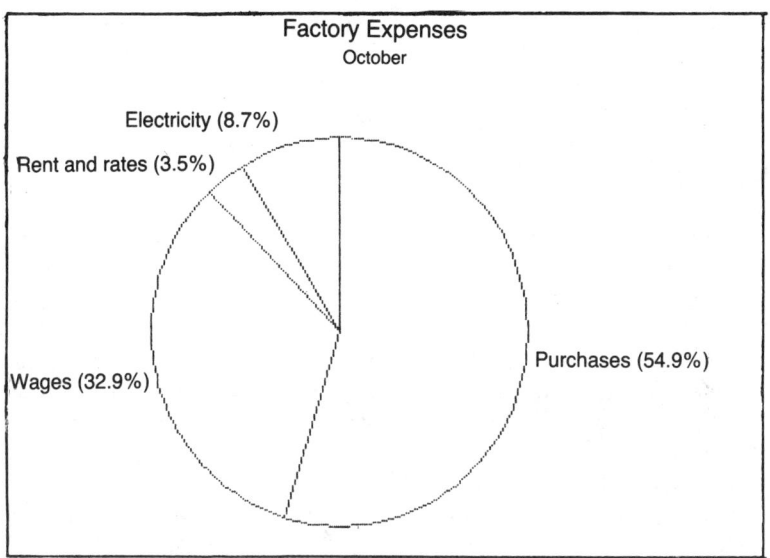

Fig. 5.9 *Bar chart from cash-flow worksheet*

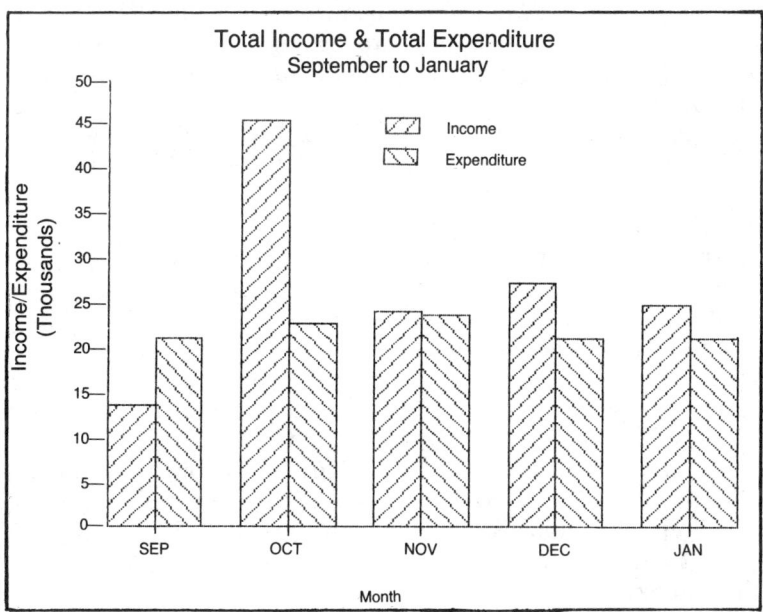

Assignment 3

Earlier in this chapter I indicated how a simple accounts system can be set up on a database package. Many small businesses, however, use spreadsheets for this task, and in this assignment you are asked to design and set up a simple accounts worksheet. This worksheet can either be for your own personal use, to record your own income and expenditure, or it can be for a fictitious business such as the one shown in Figure 5.5.

Your worksheet should resemble the conventional cashbook used by small businesses, with columns at the left to record each item of income under its appropriate heading, and columns at the right to do the same for each item of expenditure.

Some purchase transactions might be split over several columns. For example, one of your purchases at a store such as Boots might cover both food and records, which you might itemise under the 'food' and 'recreation' columns in your personal accounts worksheet. It's a good idea, therefore, to have a column at the right of your various expenses columns to show the total transaction value of these individual itemised amounts. A similar column should be provided at the right of the income columns. (This follows the convention used in ordinary cashbooks.)

At the foot of your worksheet you should provide a row showing the totals of each column. Don't forget to leave plenty of empty rows above this in which to enter your transactions. There should also be a cell in your worksheet to calculate the cash balance (i.e. the difference between the total income and the total expenditure).

As part of the design task you should insert formulae in the various totals cells and in the cash balance cell, so that the calculations are carried out automatically. You will need to test these formulae with some trial data.

When everything is working correctly, you should 'go live', i.e. enter some transactions. When you have entered a reasonable number of transactions, you should use your spreadsheet's graphing facility to produce a pie chart and a bar chart. These should illustrate the main features of your data, such as the relative sizes of the various totals in the expenditure section of your worksheet.

For this assignment, you should hand in to your tutor a print-out of your worksheet and your charts. You should also hand in a brief report summarising the advantages and disadvantages of using a spreadsheet rather than a database package for keeping these accounts.

Questions

1 Your tutor could keep his student records on either a database management package or a spreadsheet. Give three advantages of using a database package for this task, and three of using a spreadsheet. What kind of package would you advise him to use?

2 Joe builds home extensions. Write down two possible database applications for his computer, and two spreadsheet applications.

3 Write down the formula that will be used in the working capital cell for November in the cash-flow worksheet in Figure 5.5.

Chapter 6
Communicating with Other Computers

Computer communications, sometimes called 'data communications', is the subject of this chapter. Over the last decade or so there has been a huge growth in this kind of communications. It is part of the *telecommunications* revolution which is so much a feature of the IT age. 'Telecommunications' means 'communications at a distance', and includes technologies like the telephone and TV.

Data communications covers three main types of task.

- Accessing data held on remote computer systems. One example is the pages of data stored on the Prestel computers. Accessing this is rather like going to a large library to look up information – the difference is your computer does the walking. A library of data stored on a computer system is called a *database*. (The record-keeping systems you met in the last chapter are a simple form of database.)
- To transfer files from one computer to another. Software can be sold in this way, and files of data can be instantly sent across the country. The process of receiving a file from a remote computer is called *downloading*; the process of sending a file to a remote computer is called *uploading*.
- Sending messages such as memos in electronic form between computers. This is called electronic mail, or *email*.

Computer communications normally take place over the public telephone lines, hence the use of the term *on-line* in this connection. We talk about 'going on-line' to describe the process of accessing a remote computer, and 'on-line database' to describe a database that is accessed in this way. However, other links are possible, ranging from simple lengths of cable connecting two computers in the same office to the latest communications satellites far out in space. These and other more

94

technical aspects of the telecommunications revolution are described in the next chapter.

In the past, computing and telecommunications were regarded as quite separate technologies. The telephone, after all, was designed for voice, and computers for data. Today, these technologies are coming together, or *converging*. This process is helped by the deployment of the silicon chip in equipment of all kinds, so that systems like the telephone and TV are gradually becoming digitised, able to speak the same language of 0s and 1s as the computer.

6.1 Why Communicate by Computer?

The three types of communications task listed above can also be carried out using other methods, such as the postal system. So why use computers for communications? There are a number of reasons.

- Most information today is held in electronic form on computer systems. It makes sense therefore to transfer this information directly over electronic links, rather than via an intermediate link such as sending it on paper through the post.
- Telecommunications systems provide for the very rapid transfer of information over long distances. Compare the instant response that you get over the phone with the delays that occur with the post.
- Modern telecommunications links allow businesses to send large amounts of data at low cost. Most of our existing telephone network is not modern, and so phone bills can be expensive. This is changing, however, one example being the fibre optic links that are starting to connect exchanges, able to transmit huge amounts of information at high speed and low cost. Computer communications are becoming cheap.
- With computers you can access remote databases, such as Prestel, *interactively*. This means that you can make requests and carry out your own searches of the database. The fast retrieval time of electronic systems ensures that the required items of information are located very quickly.

6.2 What Do You Need for Remote Communications?

Almost all communications between remote computers (as distinct from computers located in the same office) take place over the telephone network. Because this network is not yet fully digitised, the digital output of the computers has to be converted to the same analogue form as the electrical waves transmitted by your telephone. To lapse into technical language for a moment, the 'carrier wave' that travels down the telephone line has to be 'modulated' with the computer signal.

(You may be familiar with the idea of carrier-wave modulation from radio and TV, where the broadcast signals are carried on radio carrier waves of particular frequencies. You tune your receiver to the particular carrier waves put out by your local station, and so pick up the broadcasts. I shall be saying more about this in Chapter 7.)

When the telephone signal is received by the destination computer, it has to be 'demodulated'. This means removing the carrier wave, leaving the original digital message that the computer understands.

So a device called a *modem*, short for 'modulator/demodulator' must sit between the computer and the telephone socket, modulating outgoing signals and demodulating incoming signals. This must be connected to the communications port (socket) at the back of the computer, through which all communications pass, and to the telephone socket. Normally, the cabling required for this is supplied with the modem. Some modems are *internal*, meaning they can be fixed inside the computer's casing.

Once the telephone network is fully digitised, modems will become unnecessary, and computers will be able to communicate directly over the phone line. When this happens, it is voice communications that will face the conversion problem: they will have to be digitised (i.e. coded in binary form) prior to transmission over the digital telephone network and then decoded at the other end. A device called a *codec* will be installed in each handset to do this.

There are a number of modems on the market, offering various features including a range of transmission/reception speeds (see opposite). A standard design, though, is that produced by the Hayes company, and many Hayes-compatible modems are now available.

One of the features offered by many modems is auto-dialling. This enables your computer to automatically dial up the remote computer, using telephone numbers stored on disk or keyed in. This is much easier than connecting a telephone to the system, dialling up from this, then operating switches and replacing the handset when connection is established.

Besides a modem, you need communications software. This does two jobs:

- it provides facilities for sending messages and files from your computer to other computers, and vice versa;
- it allows you to adjust the way in which your computer sends and receives data so that it matches the way that the remote computer receives and sends.

This latter task — matching communications characteristics or *protocols* — is explained below. The software carries it out by making electronic adjustments to the modem's settings. Because of the range of modems that are available, this software may incorporate modem *drivers*, i.e. additional programs that match the software's output to the characteristics of the modem. It's worth pointing out that almost all business communications packages support the Hayes modem standard, either directly or via a driver, so it makes sense to purchase this kind of modem.

6.3 Setting Up for Communications

Computers use a common communications standard called RS-232. This specifies a number of parameters, including the physical connections used in the communications port of the computer, and the fact that the data is to be communicated *serially*, i.e. one bit at a time. It doesn't specify a single speed at which the data is to be communicated, but instead specifies a number of possible speeds.

These speeds are measured in bits per second, or *baud* (pronounced 'bode'). The possible baud rates are:

75, 150, 300, 600, 1200, 2400, 4800, 9600

and upwards. As you can see, the rate doubles at every step.

Bearing in mind that a bit is a binary 0 or 1, and a byte (8 bits) represents one character, you can roughly work out how fast each of the above baud rates will transmit a piece of text. It is not quite as fast as the answer you get by dividing these numbers by 8, as there are one or two extra bits added on to each byte during data communications which are used for data checking and other purposes (see below).

It is quicker, and therefore cheaper, to send data at high baud rates. The problem is that at the higher speeds, corruption of the data is more likely to occur, so that the message gets scrambled.

Modern telecommunications links allow high transmission rates, though the lower rates of 300 baud and 1200 baud are still commonly used.

Communications software allows you to select any of these baud rates, automatically adjusting the modem's reception/transmission speeds. Note, though, that your modem may not be capable of all these possible speeds. In fact, it may only work at rates of up to 1200 baud or possibly 2400 baud, in which case you are limited to those settings only.

Computer communications are in two directions ('transmit' and 'receive'), and the baud rates for the two do not necessarily have to be the same. If you access the Prestel database, for example, you will receive data from Prestel at 1200 baud, but transmit at 75 baud. (This means, of course, that the Prestel computer is receiving at 75 baud and transmitting at 1200 baud.) This split baud rate is written 1200/75. For most communications, baud rates of 300/300, 1200/1200, or 2400/2400 are used. In these cases, the receive and transmit rates are the same.

Besides the baud rate, other protocols that have to be set include:

- *start/stop bit* protocol, which specifies how bits are to be added to a byte to indicate to the receiving computer the beginning and end of a character;
- *parity*, which is a method of checking, by means of an additional 'check' bit, that the byte has been received correctly. (One parity protocol adds a 0 if the number of 0s in the byte is even, and a 1 if the number is odd. The receiving computer checks the parity bit for correctness; if it is wrong, corruption of data has occurred, and it will send a message to the transmitting computer to send the byte again.)

If you find this complicated, you are not alone. Getting communications going on my computer was quite the trickiest thing I have ever had to do with it. Now that I have got the software and the modem up and running, however, communications are quite effortless. The reasons why it works so easily in practice are as follows:

- for most computer communications, a standard range of settings is used, so you rarely have to trouble yourself with anything other than ensuring that the baud rate is correct;
- some modems will even automatically adjust the baud rate for you, by analysing the signal received from the other computer;
- communications software allows you to automate many of your communications tasks.

To illustrate this last point, and show how easy and automatic computer communications can be, let me tell you about my bank account which I can access from my computer over Prestel. I can select 'bank account' from the menu of choices that appears when I switch my computer on, and after prompting for a password (a security measure I have added), it does the following tasks without me having to lift a finger:

- it runs my communications software;
- it selects Prestel from the list of systems stored by the software, automatically setting the required baud rates, etc. and dialling it up via the modem;
- after a few seconds, when connection is established, it enters my Prestel account number and password, so getting into the Prestel system;
- it then immediately accesses the Prestel 'gateway' to my bank's computer;
- after a second or two, when access is established, it enters my bank account number and my password;
- it then pauses while I type in a four-digit transaction number from the list sent by my bank (a security feature);
- it finally displays my bank statement in readiness for any other transactions I might wish to carry out via my computer, such as paying bills.

This whole process takes under a minute, and makes tasks such as paying for my electricity, gas, and other bills much easier than by traditional methods (though not, unfortunately, any less painful).

6.4   What Do You Need for Local Communications?

By 'local communications', I mean communications within an office or a building. For this you need just a cable connecting the computers (via their communications ports) and suitable software.

In the simplest case of communications between only two computers, you can run the communications software used for the remote communications described in the last section. This software normally includes facilities for handling a two-way local link. In the more complex case of a number of computers linked together by a local area network (LAN), special networking systems software is required.

Networking has a number of benefits, which I outlined in Chapter 2 – electronic mail, sharing files and resources, etc. Why, though, should anyone want to set up communications between just two computers in an office? The main reason, in fact, is to transfer files between two incompatible computers.

I have an old BBC microcomputer stuck in a corner in my study. This is now mainly used by my son for games, but it has another very serious use: as a machine for keying in text when my PC is busy. My wife does a fair bit of writing, and there are times when we both need a keyboard. One of us will then use the Wordwise word processor on the Beeb. BBC disks cannot be read by a PC, as the two machines are incompatible; however, transferring the files across to the PC is no problem using a cable linking the machines.

- First, the Wordwise text is saved as an ASCII file.
- Next, it is transferred to the PC using communications software (see below).
- Finally, it is read into a word processing program on the PC using its 'import' option.

The whole transfer process takes just two or three minutes.

The most popular communications package for setting up this kind of link is Kermit. (Yes, it was named after the frog, presumably because with it a file can jump from one machine to another.) Kermit is available for almost every kind of computer, ranging from many of the home computers up to mainframes, and with it you can pass data between any two machines (assuming, that is, that you have a suitable cable linking their communications ports). And the good news is that it's free. It is available in this country from the Kermit Distribution Service at Lancaster University.

I use Kermit for the file transfers described above. I run the BBC version of Kermit on my BBC micro, and the PC version on my PC. After issuing a couple of simple commands telling Kermit to use an appropriate (fast) baud rate and giving the name of the ASCII file that I want transferred, I sit back while the data speeds across to the PC.

6.5   On-line Databases and Bulletin Boards

Files can be transferred between remote computers in much the same way. File transfer is not the only reason for remote computer communications, though. A second important reason is to access databases, and a third is to send and receive email. Businessmen away from base often need to access their firm's main computer for these reasons, to look up data and messages, and to pass on their own data and messages.

Besides firms' own private systems, a large number of public systems are available that anyone can access. Many of these provide electronic mail facilities, databases of various types, and the facility to download files.

Public systems can be grouped into three broad classes.

- One class provides mainly commercial databases for business users together with electronic mail facilities. Prestel is one example, providing a wide range of information from 'Health & Safety at Work' information to *Which?* reports and economic statistics. The ability of the system to support electronic conferences (see below) and to download files of software is of much smaller importance, though the email/telex facilities are useful.

- Another class provides 'conferencing' facilities, allowing users to exchange news and views and to seek advice from others with similar interests. Database information is of smaller importance in these systems. The main UK conferencing system is CIX, short for 'Compulink Information Xchange'. There are a large number of conferences available on CIX, mostly computer-oriented, ranging from conferences on particular software packages to programming and advice on modems.

- The third class is called 'bulletin boards'. These are much smaller systems, many run from home by a single enthusiastic 'sysop' (system operator). Unlike the other two classes, these are often free, so that all you pay is the cost of the phone call. These are usually computer-oriented, concentrating on particular hardware systems (such as the PC, the Mac, or the Atari ST), and they are rather like electronic notice boards (hence their name). Articles of interest to owners of these machines can be perused, there is normally a 'chat' facility where people can leave messages, and software may be available for downloading.

To use an on-line database or conferencing system, you normally have to pay a monthly subscription fee plus a per-minute charge for usage. On top of this there may be a small charge for accessing certain items in the database. Then, of course, there is the cost of the phone call, though for many systems this will be charged at local call rates.

Prestel and CIX are relatively cheap, as these are aimed at members of the public as well as businesses, and your total monthly bill for these will probably be around £5 per month (depending on usage) plus phone charges at local rates. Other systems, aimed at businesses and researchers, are generally more expensive, and some cost upwards of £150 per hour of usage.

6.6   Electronic Mail

Most of these systems provide email facilities, allowing subscribers to send messages to each other. The advantages of email over the conventional post are outlined below.

- It is immediate, as the messages arrive in the recipient's electronic mailbox the instant they are sent.
- It can be cheaper. In an email session lasting about 20 minutes it is possible to deal with around 20 messages – reading letters, sending replies, forwarding copies to others, deleting or filing the correspondence – often at local call rates.
- Being computer-controlled, it allows subscribers to do things which would be difficult or expensive by traditional mail. For example, you can send the same message to a group of subscribers, or all subscribers, at the press of a key. (Unfortunately, advertisers on Prestel have latched on to this capability, and regularly fill up everyone's mailbox with junk mail.)

Email systems work by assigning to each user an area of storage on the host computer on which incoming mail is stored. This is his *mailbox*. Each subscriber has an ID which is attached to this mailbox. On some systems, such as CIX, this is his name, on others it may be an ID number. In the case of Prestel, it is the subscriber's phone number.

To send a message, you must therefore know the recipient's ID. Normally, you will have a note of people with whom you regularly correspond, but all systems provide indexes of subscribers (rather like a phone directory) that you can look up. The email procedure is just like writing a letter: you enter the recipient's email address (i.e. his or her ID), type the message, and press the key that will instantly send it over the phone to his or her mailbox on the host computer.

To look at your own mailbox, you move to it either via a menu system (as in Prestel), or by typing a command such as 'Mail' (as in CIX). You can then read your stored incoming mail, and either leave it in your mailbox for future reference, or else delete it. Most systems allow you to store up to a certain number of read messages.

6.7   The Controlling Software

On-line databases, conferencing systems, and bulletin boards are controlled by software. The purpose of this software is to organise and store the database or conference material, and the email correspondence, and to allow subscribers to find their way through it to the parts that interest them. The software makes use of the computer's lightning-fast ability to perform searches and other tasks. So it enables users to search for database items which contain keywords of interest, for example.

Some software packages for these systems are menu-driven, others are command-driven. Menu-driven systems are easy to master and use; command-driven systems are more difficult, but they give the user more power and flexibility. The features of both are described below.

a) A menu-driven system — Prestel
A good example of a menu-driven system is Prestel. Prestel information is stored in about 300 000 *frames* or *pages*, each one equivalent to a 40-column computer screen (i.e. having 40 characters across instead of 80). Figure 6.1 shows a Prestel frame; it is in fact an *index frame*, or menu, which leads to further frames when you key one of the numbers listed at the right.

Fig. 6.1   *A Prestel frame*

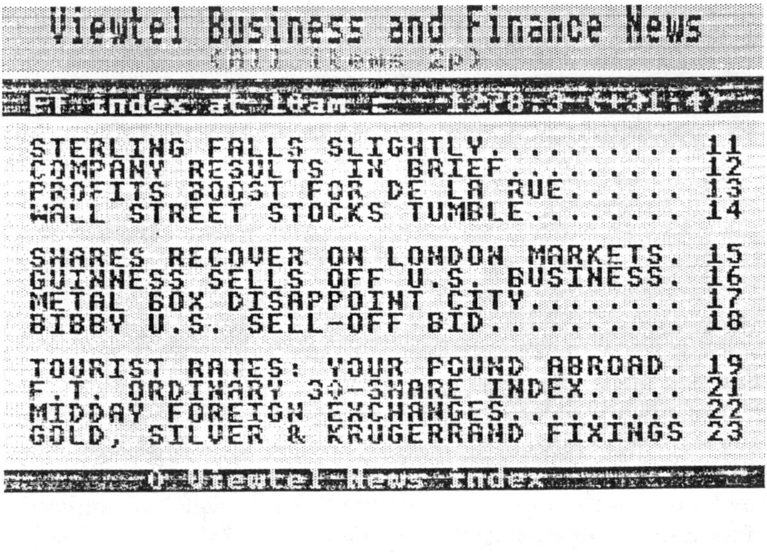

(Prestel frames are similar to the ones you see on your TV if you can receive Ceefax or Oracle. The particular display system employed, with its chunky graphics, is called *teletext*. I will be saying more about this in Chapter 7. Note that Prestel and similar systems are called *viewdata* or sometimes *videotex* systems, and the collection of frames that make up such a system is called a *viewdatabase*.)

Prestel frames are organised into a hierarchy of major areas, each one subdivided into topics, sub-topics, and so on down through many levels. Figure 6.2 illustrates this, showing the organisation of pages in a Prestel-like viewdata system that I once set up on a computer network to provide users with information on major IT topics. Each of the boxes in the figure represents an index frame (i.e. a menu), and the arrows below the boxes indicate that there are further frames containing the subject-matter to which these menus refer.

Fig. 6.2   *Menu system for a small viewdatabase*

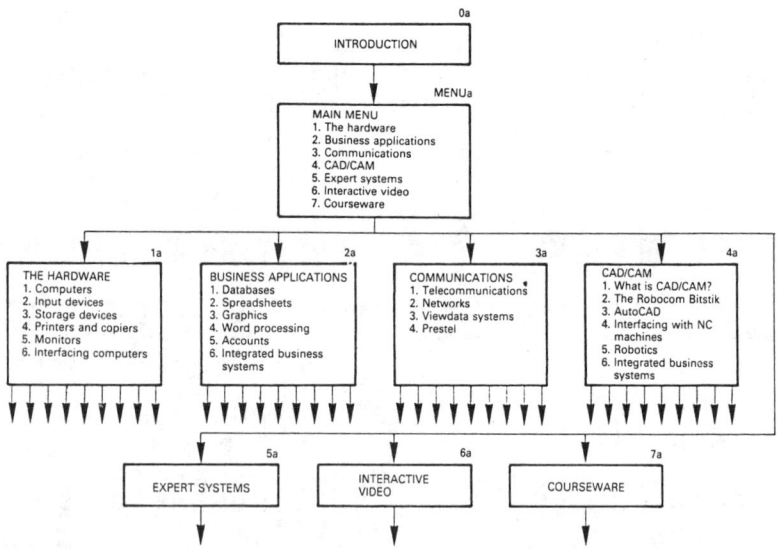

A frame is linked electronically to other related frames to provide the routeing system. For example, if you are at the main index frame towards the top of Figure 6.2, pressing '1' will route you to the 'Hardware' index, and pressing '1' again will take you to the frames describing computers.

So in the case of Prestel, starting at the main index you keep pressing numbers to move through successive indexes till you reach the frame, or sequence of frames, that you require. At any time the system allows you to move back up through your route via earlier indexes, usually by pressing the number 0.

This kind of menu system is rather long-winded, but fortunately there are ways of by-passing it and moving directly to your destination frames.

- One way is to call up a frame by keying in its number – each of the hundreds of thousands of frames has a unique number. Most users of Prestel keep a list of frame numbers that they frequently access, and the Prestel directory gives the frame numbers of many index frames.
- A second way involves keying in the name of the topic you wish to look up. Typing 'education', for example, takes you directly to the main education database in Prestel.

A description of some of the facilities available on Prestel is given later.

b) A command-driven system – CIX
The Compulink Information Xchange is a good example of a command-driven system. It is controlled by the CoSy (Conferencing System) software. Unlike the viewdata systems described above, CoSy (in common with most other on-line systems) uses an 80-column screen display, the information being presented as continuously scrolling text instead of being split up into individual frames.

If a user types the CoSy command 'show all', for example, the software will list all conferences with a one-line description of each. There are many dozens of such commands; here's a list of just a few:

Help   – display a list of commands with some explanatory comments.
Show Microtext – give details of the Microtext conference.
Join Microtext – join the Microtext conference.
<CR>   – i.e. press Enter – this displays the conference messages one at a time.
Skip to 25   – skip to message number 25.
Say   – add a message of your own to the conference.
Comment   – comment on the last message read.
Quit   – leave a conference.

Mail	– go to your email area in the system.
Status	– see what email is there.
12	– read letter number 12.
To rcarter	– write a message to R Carter.
Send	– send the message.
Bye	– leave the conferencing system.

6.8   Examples of On-line Databases

There is a wealth of information held on computer databases throughout the world, much of it instantly available to businesses and research workers. Furthermore, because this information is in electronic form, it is much more likely to be kept up-to-date than information that is printed in a book.

There are, in fact, some 2000 major on-line databases, so the chances are that somewhere on this planet there is a host computer connected to a phone line that has that vital bit of information that you need. The problem is, which one? Fortunately, directories of databases are available. Furthermore, many of these on-line systems provide lists of other databases with an indication of their subject areas, and they may provide gateways – i.e. electronic links – to those databases, so that users can transfer across to them.

This section describes just three of the many commercial on-line database and email systems that are available.

a) Dialog
One of the largest and most widely-used on-line databases is the American Dialog database. It covers a wide range of subject areas, including:

Agriculture and nutrition
Bibliography (i.e. books and monographs)
Business and economics
Chemistry
Current affairs
Directories
Education
Energy and environment
Foundations and grants
Law and government
Material sciences
Medicines and biosciences
Multidisciplinary

On-line training and practice
Patents and trademarks
Science and technology
Social science and humanities.

b) Prestel

Prestel is run by the Dialcom division of British Telecom. It is the main UK viewdata system, with some 90 000 subscribers and many information providers (IPs) who contribute the frames. There are a huge number of topics on Prestel, though the information covered in many of them often doesn't amount to much.

To give you an idea of what's on offer, here's what the Prestel main index looks like:

```
P R E S T E L              1a              0p
Main Index
━━━━━━━━━━━━━━━━━━━━━━━━━━━━━━━━━━━━━━━━━━━
1 FOCUS           POST STRIKE VIEWS
New  Mix  messages,games,entertainment,  Full
Olympic schedule,Connexions news
━━━━━━━━━━━━━━━━━━━━━━━━━━━━━━━━━━━━━━━━━━━
20 AGRICULTURE     24 INSURANCE
21 BANKING         25 MICROCOMPUTING
22 BUSINESS        26 TELESHOPPING
23 EDUCATION       27 TRAVEL
━━━━━━━━━━━━━━━━━━━━━━━━━━━━━━━━━━━━━━━━━━━
5 MESSAGE SERVICES Mailbox,Telex Link
6 NEWS, WEATHER, LEISURE, SPORT
━━━━━━━━━━━━━━━━━━━━━━━━━━━━━━━━━━━━━━━━━━━
7 A-Z INDEXES to information & IPs
8 CUSTOMER GUIDE All about Prestel
9 WHAT'S NEW 6th SEPTEMBER
━━━━━━━━━━━━━━━━━━━━━━━━━━━━━━━━━━━━━━━━━━━
```

Each one of these options leads to further menus and sub-menus, providing in total many thousands of topics. These topics are, in effect, small viewdatabases, and most of them are run by independent IPs. They may make a small per-frame charge to cover costs, or they may run their databases as closed user groups (see next page) and charge a subscription to those who belong.

Besides these viewdatabases, Prestel offers a number of other services.

- A mailbox service. Owing to the limited amount of information that can be held on a viewdata screen, this is suitable for short messages only. However, it is linked to the telex system (see Chapter 7), so that messages can be sent to any of the millions of telex subscribers worldwide.
- 'Chatting' facilities, a form of simple conferencing, i.e. areas where subscribers can leave messages for others to read and, if they wish, to reply to.
- Teleshopping, i.e. facilities to read about and order goods and services.
- Closed user groups (CUGs). These are specialist areas within Prestel which are not accessible to the ordinary user. To belong to a CUG, you normally have to pay a membership fee. The most well-known Prestel CUG is Micronet, which provides microcomputer information, software, and a chatting service.
- Gateways providing access to other computers. If you belong to the Nottingham Building Society's 'Homelink' CUG, for example, then you can access your account via a gateway to their computer.

c) Telecom Gold
Telecom 'Gold' (also from British Telecom) is a more up-to-date system than Prestel, with sophisticated email facilities and gateways to a number of databases. These include *World Reporter* (which offers abstracts of financial publications such as the Financial Times), *OAG* (the official airlines guide), and *IDB Online* (for computer information).

Other services include a bulletin board, telex facilities, and radiopaging (so that the recipient of your message can be warned by his bleeper sounding).

Questions

1 How many pages of text can be transmitted in ten seconds at 19 200 baud? Assume 500 words per page and five characters per word.

2 Your monthly budget is sufficient to allow you to join either the Micronet CUG on Prestel or the CIX conferencing system. Give two advantages of joining Micronet and two of joining CIX.

3 Give three advantages of electronic mail over the ordinary post. Try to think of two disadvantages.

4 Give three advantages to the researcher of using on-line databases rather than a university or other library.

Chapter 7

Telecommunications

Computers and telecommunications are the twin pillars of the IT revolution. Computer technology enables us to capture, store, retrieve, process, and output information; telecommunications technology enables us to communicate information to every part of the globe and deep into space.

In the past, the two were quite separate, the first being based on the digital technology of the silicon chip and the second using the analogue (wave-like) technology of the telephone and radio. Today they are converging, with the telephone network becoming digitised, and digital radio and TV being forecast for the near future. The latest telecommunications developments – such as fibre optic cables – are digital.

One result of this is that all electronic equipment, from the computer to the TV and the telephone network, will one day be able to be linked directly together without the need for expensive adaptors such as modems.

This chapter surveys the telecommunications scene, introducing you to the technology and to some of the wide range of services that are now on offer.

7.1 What is Telecommunications?

Telecommunications, or 'telecoms' for short, means 'communications at a distance'. Ever since the development of the morse code, these communications have been based upon waves travelling along a wire or through space. In the case of the telephone, electrical waves travel along the wire, in the case of radio, radio waves travel through the air or through space.

To transmit speech, a single-frequency *carrier wave* is *modulated* with the waveform of the speech. What this means is that the speech waveform is superimposed on the carrier wave for transmission purposes. At the receiver, the carrier wave is removed, leaving the original speech. TV and other signals are transmitted in the same way.

One way of modulating the carrier wave is *amplitude modulation*. In this, the frequency of the carrier wave is not altered by the waveform of the speech, but its amplitude is. Figure 7.1 illustrates the principle behind this kind of modulation, but don't worry if you don't understand it.

Fig. 7.1 *Amplitude modulation*

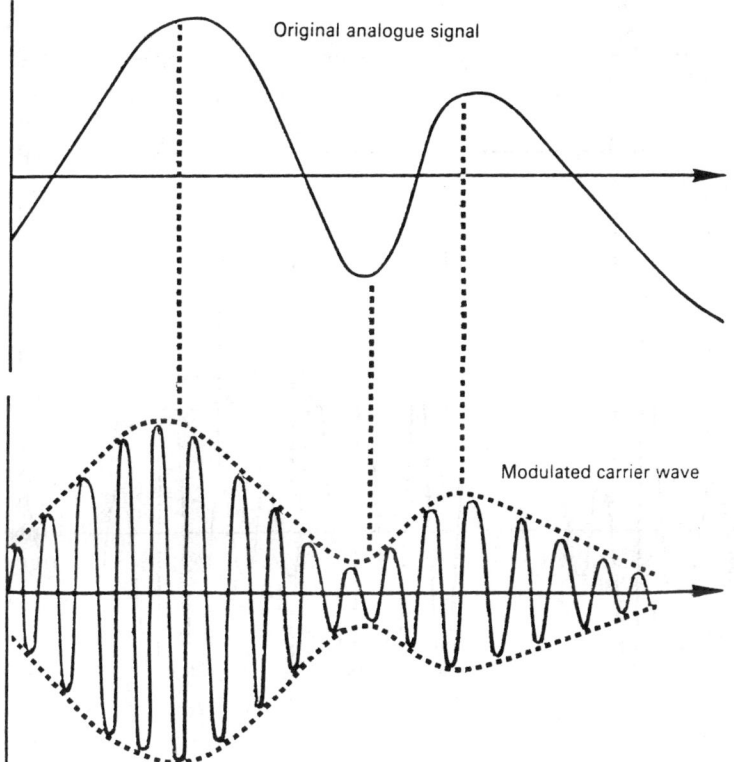

Radio broadcasts on the short wave, medium wave, and long wave bands are 'AM' (i.e. amplitude modulated). Your radio receiver can pick up many hundreds of such broadcasts – you select the one you want by tuning to the frequency of the carrier wave, and the radio then extracts from it the broadcast message.

The signals that a computer generates and which pass along its internal circuitry are not like this. As you learned earlier on, they are digital pulses of electricity, representing binary 0s and 1s. To communicate this type of information over the telephone line, a modem has to superimpose the digital characteristics of the signal on the carrier wave. One way of doing this is by amplitude modulation, and Figure 7.2 illustrates how the digital pulses (at the top of the figure) are converted to different amplitudes of the carrier wave.

Fig. 7.2   *Amplitude modulation by a digital signal*

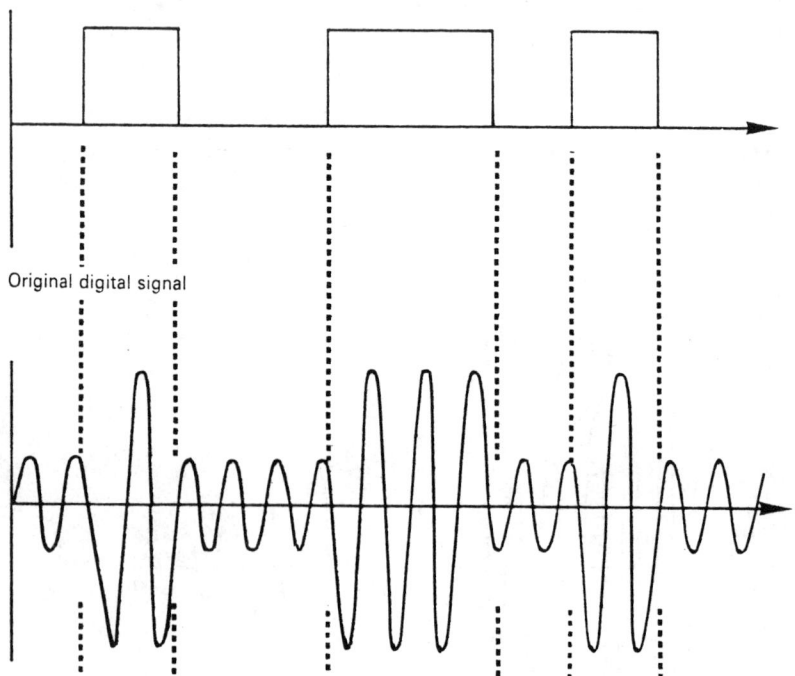

Original digital signal

Modulated carrier wave

Not all communications links transmit information by means of carrier waves. Local area networks, for instance, are entirely digital (so modems are not required for networking), and some parts of the telephone network are also digital.

7.2   Broadband Communications

Fibre optic cables are one example of a digital communications link. These are being laid down in many countries, including our own, to link major telephone exchanges. They are also being used to carry TV transmissions from satellite reception dishes to people's homes. These cables carry information as pulses of laser light.

The advantage of using this kind of link is not just that it brings telecoms closer to the digital world of computers. It is the enormous volume of communications that these links can carry.

The capacity of a communications link is called its *bandwidth*. This measures the amount of information that can pass through it in a second. In the case of analogue communications, such as over the telephone, the bandwidth is the range of frequencies that can pass through the link. In the case of digital communications it is the number of bits per second that can travel through it.

(In the analogue case, the bandwidth is measured in KHz. 1 KHz = 1000 Hertz, and 1 Hertz = 1 cycle per second. Human speech covers a frequency range from around 50 Hz to 12 KHz, whereas the bandwidth of a telephone line is only about 4 KHz. That's why speech over the telephone, although perfectly intelligible, loses so much of its frequency range and therefore its quality.)

The bandwidth of an optical fibre is vastly greater than that of an ordinary telephone wire. This means that:

● more messages can be transmitted at the same time along the link;
● each message can cover a much wider frequency range.

A single fibre optic cable can carry almost half the (voice) phone calls being made at any one time in the country. Or it can carry several TV transmissions (these cover a much wider frequency range than speech and therefore require a much greater bandwidth.)

Communications links with a wide bandwidth are called *broadband* links.

7.3   Advantages of Digital Communications

Besides these benefits offered by digital links such as fibre optic cabling, the digitisation of the telephone and other telecommunications networks has other advantages.

● One advantage is the fact that all information – whether voice, image, text, or data – is sent in a common digital form that can be handled by computer-based equipment. Every kind of transmission, whether phone, video, or computer data, can share the same system. *ISDN*, short for 'integrated services digital network', is the name given to this new type of system. As explained earlier, carrier waves can be used to carry digital information, which is why ISDN can use radio waves and other analogue links.

- Since the information can be handled by computer, a number of new services are possible. British Telecom's digital service offers over 50 new facilities that were not previously available.
- Information in digital form is less prone to noise and degradation than information in analogue (wave) form. This is because a pulse is easily recognised as such by the equipment handling it, and can be separated from the accompanying noise. (As an example of degradation, think what happens to a recording on cassette tape when you record it to another tape, and then from this to a third tape. The quality drops appreciably. In the case of a digital record, for example a computer file stored on magnetic disk, there is no such degradation – you can copy through endless generations without any quality loss.)

7.4   Services Provided by the Telephone Network

Businesses are connected electronically to the outside world by the telephone network. All sorts of hi-tech links may form part of that network – such as optic fibres and communications satellites – but the user is unaware of them. He or she is concerned with everyday pieces of equipment like the telephone handset and the fax machine, and the range of services associated with these. This section aims to cover the most important of these.

a) The telephone
The telephone for voice communications has been with us for a long time, and it will survive into the foreseeable future. What's new (or newish) is the following range of associated equipment and services.

- Answering machines for receiving and recording incoming calls.
- Handsets offering features such as a memory for storing and dialling frequently-used numbers and an automatic redial facility for engaged numbers.
- Computer-based facilities offered by telecommunications authorities, such as automatic ring-back and tracing of malicious calls.

- Telephone conferencing so that several parties can be linked together in a single call (see later).
- Cellular radio so that phones can be used in a moving vehicle (see below).

Some new services being developed for some subscribers in America but not yet available in this country are listed below.

- Transmission of the caller's telephone number, so that it appears on a screen attached to the recipient's phone. This enables the latter to choose to answer, reject, or forward the call to another number.
- *Call block*, allowing recipients to program their phones to automatically reject calls from up to twelve known numbers.
- *Priority screening*, which gives priority treatment to calls from up to twelve selected numbers – the phone rings in a distinctive way when a priority number calls, and if the recipient is out, the number is stored in the telephone company's computer for later access by the recipient.
- *Call forwarding*, which automatically switches all calls or pre-selected calls to another number.
- *Call answering*, which works rather like an answering machine. Subscribers can leave a prerecorded message on the telephone company's computer, which is automatically relayed to callers. They in turn can leave messages for the subscriber.

b) Cellular radio
Cellular radio is a computer-controlled mobile communications service made possible by digital communications technology. Under this system, cellular radio sets, or mobiles, normally installed in cars, can communicate with one another and with ordinary phone users in the following way.

The country is split up into a large number of cells, each one between two and twenty miles across (depending on whether it is in a rural or urban area), and having at its centre a base with a low-powered radio transmitter. This is able to transmit to and receive from any mobiles within the perimeter of the cell, and it is connected via a computer-controlled switching centre to the telephone network. Outside the perimeter of the cell the strength of the signal rapidly fades, so that although bases in adjacent cells use different radio frequencies, one in a non-adjacent cell can use the same frequencies without risk of interference.

When a cellular radio subscriber keys in a telephone number on his mobile, it is transmitted over a special control channel to the cell base, which passes it to the switching centre. The centre dials the number on the telephone network, and at the same time allocates a radio frequency to the mobile, which automatically switches to that frequency and so enables the user to make the call. If he drives his vehicle from one cell to another while the call is in progress, the switching centre automatically switches transmitters and frequencies.

In the case of calls made to a mobile, the switching centre sends a paging signal on the control channel. The system will switch the paging transmission from cell to cell until it locates the set, the search being done in an intelligent manner by contacting first the set's home base and looking up the computer records of its last known location. The search time is never more than a few seconds.

c) Telex

Telex is a popular way of transmitting text over the telephone network, though for reasons which are explained below it is facing a strong challenge from facsimile.

Telex is transmitted and received by *teletypewriters*, which are a kind of communicating typewriter with a paper tape punch and a paper tape reader. Contact between two teletypes is established by dialling in the usual way, and the text may then be typed in to the transmitting teletype by the telex operator. However, in order to save on telephone line time, the message will normally be typed in and recorded on paper tape before the call takes place, and then read rapidly from the tape after dial-up.

Most major organisations are telex users, and the service boasts over a million subscribers worldwide. Two factors have contributed to this success:

- all telex machines observe common communications protocols, i.e. they are all compatible;
- there is a comprehensive directory of telex users.

In the future, however, other text communication services are likely to supersede telex, the reason being that its transmission rate is low (50 baud, i.e. about a word per second), which means that the length of each call, and therefore the phone charge, is relatively high.

d) Teletex

Teletex (not to be confused with teletext) is an enhanced telex system designed to take advantage of modern digital telecommunications systems. The transmission rate is 2400 baud, almost 50 times faster than telex. Although this system is expected eventually to take over from telex, its current usage is low because teletex standards have not been precisely specified, so there is some incompatibility between different manufacturers' machines.

e) Facsimile

Facsimile, or *fax* for short, was developed at the beginning of this century to transmit images, such as newspaper photographs, by telephone line. A fax machine contains a photoelectric cell which scans the image and converts the blacks, greys, and whites into electrical signals, which modulate the telephone carrier wave. The same device will also act as a receiver, able to decode incoming signals and print them as image on special paper. Nowadays, the 'images' that are transmitted by fax are often pages of text.

Fax machines are grouped according to quality of scanning and reproduction. Group 1 machines give high quality results, with good differentiation between the various shades of grey. The amount of information that has to be transmitted in this case is high, and so the transmission time for an A4 document is a lengthy six minutes. Group 2 machines give lower quality results but cut the transmission time in half.

Of most interest so far as text transmission is concerned are the Group 3 and 4 machines, which give black and white results without grey tones. Unlike Group 1 and 2, these are digital machines, converting a black (or dark grey) dot on paper to a binary 1, and a white (or light grey) dot to a binary 0. They are well suited to digital communications, and the transmission time – and therefore the cost of each call – is very low. Current models are about the size of a small dot matrix printer, they cost around £1000, and they can transmit an A4 page in just a few seconds.

In the past, the use of fax was inhibited by:

- the lack of a directory of users;
- the fact that fax machines differed in widely in their transmission rates, so that one manufacturer's models could not communicate with those of another.

Today, however, there is a directory of users, and the digital Group 3 and 4 machines have standardised transmission rates. This, and the high transmission speeds, have brought about the boom in fax usage.

f) Videophones and videoconferencing

Nowadays, it is possible to see as well as hear a telephone caller by using a *videophone*, a device consisting of both a video system and a phone. The video system consists of a black-and-white video camera and a monitor.

An ordinary black-and-white video picture uses the same bandwidth as 600 telephone conversations. To avoid prohibitively expensive calls, videophone systems transmit pictures intermittently, to give a series of still images rather than a continuously moving one. Also, they remove redundant information from the picture and use compression techniques to reduce the information that has to be sent. The system can be used, for example, to send pictures of components for fault diagnosis, pictures of damaged parts of a patient's body in the health care field, or pictures of products in the field of retailing.

Video conferencing systems are also available, which allow several callers to hold meetings without needing to travel long distances. British Telecom's Confravision system provides this sort of service, linking major cities by a network of videoconferencing studios for remote meetings.

7.5 Services Provided by the TV Network

Although TV is an important element of the IT revolution, it is not the TV broadcasts themselves that concern a book of this nature. Rather, our concern is with the ancillary services that are of value to commerce, namely Ceefax and Oracle.

Ceefax, from the BBC, and Oracle, from the IBA, are teletext transmissions that can be picked up on home TV sets that have suitable adaptors. The system has a superficial resemblance to Prestel and other viewdata systems (described in Chapter 6). This is because the information transmitted is stored on a computer system in the form of frames which, like the Prestel frames, fit a computer screen (in 40-column mode) and use teletext graphics.

Unlike Prestel, however, the TV teletext system is not interactive, i.e. it does not allow you to communicate with the transmitter to make your own selection of frames from its database. You can only passively accept frames in the broadcast sequence. This means of course, that the system is much more limited than Prestel, able to store and transmit far fewer frames. It also means, however, that the system is free, and there is in fact quite a range of business information – such as share prices – that is available on this service yet which costs money if accessed via Prestel.

Ceefax and Oracle work like this (see Figure 7.3). The frames are broadcast along with the ordinary TV signals on Channels 1, 2, 3, and 4. (So there are two Ceefax channels, namely BBC1 Ceefax and BBC2 Ceefax, and likewise two Oracle channels.) The transmission rate is so fast (7 Mbit/sec) that they can be slotted in the narrow gaps between each TV frame. (You can in fact sometimes see the transmission as a line of pulsing spots at the top of the TV picture.)

The frames are grouped into sets, each of which has a frame number. There are about 100 sets on each channel, and typically three or four frames in each set. On one channel the sets might be numbered 100-199, on another 200-299, and so on. Individual frames within a set are distinguished by adding a letter (a, b, c, etc.) to the number. The frames are broadcast in sequence as a *carousel*. It takes less than a minute to reach the end of the carousel, and then it starts from the beginning again.

The user selects the frame from the carousel he or she wants to display on the TV screen by keying in the frame's number on a keypad and then waiting for a few seconds for the carousel to reach that frame. Some frames are index frames, giving the numbers of subsidiary frames and thus providing a menu route through the information. Computer output in the form of software or files of text or data can also be sent over teletext systems, and the BBC does in fact transmit free 'telesoftware' in this way.

Fig. 7.3   *The teletext broadcasting system*

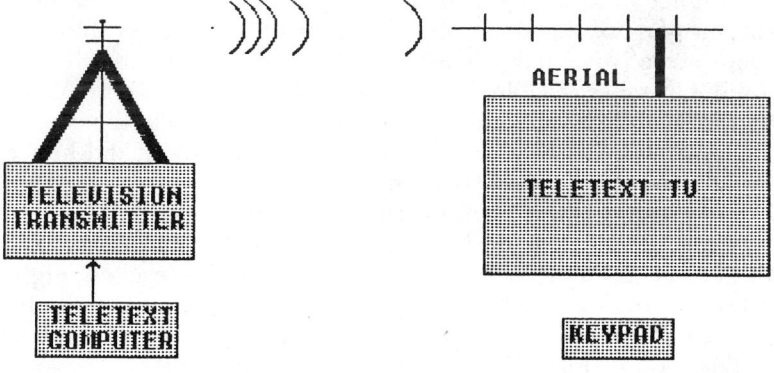

Some three million people are estimated to make use of Ceefax and Oracle. The topics covered include the weather, sport, TV programs, news, share prices, and investment advice. As on

Prestel, the information is kept up-to-date by the staff who create the frames.

7.6 Communications Satellites

In the past, telecommunications to distant parts of the earth were sent by short-wave radio. If you have tuned in to radio broadcasts from other countries you will realise how poor the reception usually is for this type of transmission. However, that it works at all is thanks to the ionosphere high in the atmosphere above the earth's surface. This reflects radio waves in the short-wave band, so that instead of passing out into space they are bounced over the horizon. They might, in fact, bounce several times between the earth and the ionosphere before reaching their final destination.

High-quality transmissions, such as are required by TV signals or computer data, must be sent via a better quality link such as cable or else VHF or UHF radio waves. (We receive local radio on VHF, TV signals on UHF. These terms mean 'very high frequency' and 'ultra-high frequency'.) However, VHF and UHF transmissions suffer from two major drawbacks:

- they tend to be blocked by natural barriers such as mountains and the curvature of the earth;
- they are not reflected by the ionosphere but pass through it into space.

To bounce such signals back to the earth, and so transmit them to distant parts of the globe, some form of reflector other than the ionosphere is needed – hence communications satellites. These are in fact more reliable than the ionosphere, which can break up at times of intense sunspot activity. They can also boost the signals they receive in order to increase their power and hence the quality of reception back on earth.

The ground-based TV/radio transmitter in this kind of link will be a large dish to beam the signal to the satellite. Much smaller dishes can be used at the receiving end; with the latest high-powered *DBS* satellites (short for 'direct broadcast satellites'), the receiving dish can be less than 1m in diameter.

These reception dishes are relatively inexpensive, for they are fixed affairs lacking any tracking facilities. A dish is able to operate in this way, pointing in only one direction, because the satellite it is picking up hangs stationary in the sky. In fact, of course, the satellite is orbiting the earth, but its speed of rotation exactly matches that of the earth.

To achieve this, communications satellites must be launched into *geostationary orbit*, which lies above the equator at 22 300 miles from the earth's surface. That's why TV reception dishes in this country point towards the southern skies. The elevation from the south of England is about 25 degrees, less from the north of England and Scotland.

One geostationary communications satellite is Intelsat, which from this country lies 25 degrees to the west of due south. It was launched in 1980 and is able to handle some 12 000 simultaneous phone calls and two TV channels. Another is the European Communications Satellite ECS-F1, which is about 13 degrees east of south, and which also carries TV broadcasts.

To pick up TV signals that are broadcast via satellite you need a dish that points in the right direction (or else a cable connected to a communal dish), and a TVRO (television receive-only) licence. You also need decoding equipment attached to your TV.

The two main TVRO satellites for Europe are Intelsat and ECS-F1. The transmissions from ECS include:

SKY	– entertainment (British)
World Net	– news and information (American)
Sat 1	– entertainment (German)
Music Box	– pop videos (Luxembourg)
TV5	– entertainment (French)
RAI	– entertainment (Italian)
Teleclub	– films (Swiss).

Besides communications satellites, there are a number of meteorological and land-surveying satellites orbiting the earth, as well as the inevitable military 'spy in the sky' reconnaissance satellites.

Assignment 4

Design a small viewdata system of your own on the subject of telecommunications. You should have a main menu with a number of choices covering topics both from this chapter and Chapter 6, and then possibly a second menu system leading to the information frames. You should draw up your design along the lines of Figure 6.2 on page 104.

Then, using the teletext design sheet shown in Figure 7.4, design in detail your opening menu frame, including teletext graphics as appropriate. If you are not familiar with teletext graphics, you should study some frames on Ceefax, Oracle, or Prestel.

Finally, write a synopsis – notes will do – of the information you will include in each of the sections of your viewdatabase. Hand in your viewdatabase design, menu frame design, and synopsis to your tutor for marking.

Fig. 7.4   *Teletext design sheet*

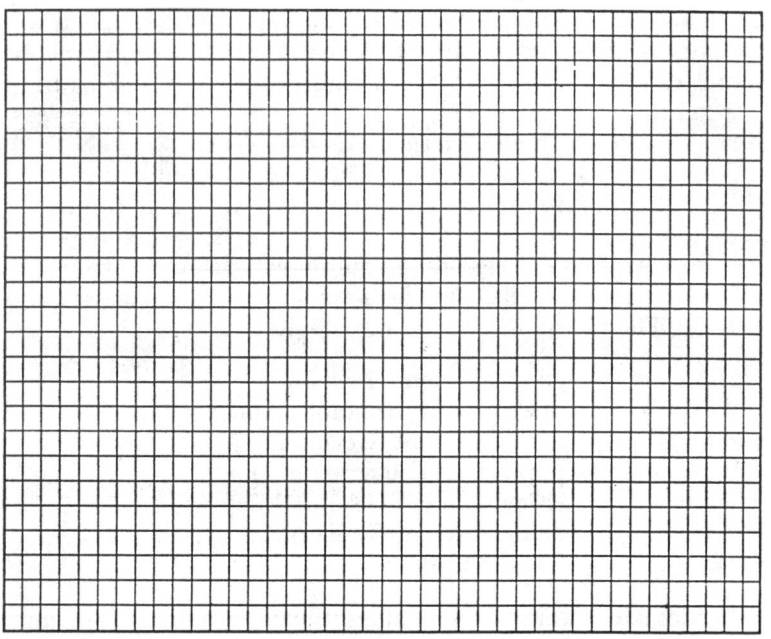

Questions

1 A number of years ago the BBC experimented with broadcasting free software over the radio in conjunction with a radio series for home computer users. The idea was that users would record it on cassette tape for loading into their computers. What technical problems do you think the home computer enthusiast would meet with this system?

2 Twenty years ago the country's telephone system could cope perfectly well without broadband communications links such as optic fibres, whereas today these are essential. What do you think has caused the big increase in traffic on the telephone lines?

3 Why are broadcasts via satellite suitable for transmitting computer data over long distances, whereas ordinary radio broadcasts are not?

4 ISDN (Integrated Systems Digital Network) allows all kinds of information to travel along the telephone network. Give two examples of the use of this for businesses.

Chapter 8

Multimedia Computing

Convergence – the coming together of different technologies – is affecting not just computing and telecommunications but several other technologies as well. Music, pictures, and many other forms of information can now be integrated and controlled by the computer, as can a variety of media such as audio and video. The term *multimedia computing* has been coined to describe this convergence of the various media technologies with computing.

This chapter examines just a few examples of this growing type of IT application. They are chosen for their relevance to the world of work and commerce, and include presentation graphics, interactive video, and compact disc. The chapter ends by looking at the impact of multimedia computing on the arts.

8.1 Presentation Graphics

In the world of the office, presentation graphics is the latest and fastest-growing type of application package. This type of package can be used to create drawings, artwork, notices, and other types of presentation. By it, lectures can be enhanced, publications made more eye-catching, and displays made more attractive.

A variety of methods for presenting the computer images produced by presentation graphics software are available.

- Laser printers can produce excellent printouts on ordinary paper or on transparencies for overhead projectors.
- The computer screen image can be photographed by a special camera to produce 35 mm slides.
- More sophisticated film recorders will convert the computer graphics file directly into a slide. This overcomes the fuzziness caused by the relatively low resolution of the computer screen.

● The computer can be connected to a large screen display for lectures and presentations, or to a special type of flat screen monitor which sits on top of an overhead projector and throws a large image onto an OHP screen.

The modules that make up this kind of package are described below. They normally make extensive use of the mouse, as this is a much better device for painting and drawing on the screen than the keyboard. The examples given are from the GEM Presentation Team package.

a) Painting
You made some use of painting software in the assignment at the end of Chapter 2. With it, you can draw freehand pictures on the screen, using lines of varying widths and colours, and to fill in (or 'paint') areas of the drawing with colours and patterns. A variety of painting 'tools' are provided by this software, and you select these by pointing with the mouse at the appropriate icon displayed in an on-screen 'toolbox'. You can select colours and patterns in a similar way from an on-screen palette.

Figure 8.1 shows the screen display from GEM Paint, showing a painting together with the toolbox and the palette. The painting tools include:

● a pencil – to draw lines;
● a spraycan – to create air-brush effects;
● an eraser – to rub out;
● a microscope – to zoom up on part of the picture in order to make very detailed and precise changes.

Clip-art libraries are also available for many painting programs. These consist of collections of drawings and artwork, produced on the computer by professional artists and designers, which can be freely added to your own pictures. They include images of people, office equipment, buildings, etc. You can also add small amounts of text to your picture.

b) Drawing software
This software is the electronic equivalent of a set of mathematical drawing instruments – a ruler, compasses, set-square, etc. With it, you can draw accurate designs of, for example, buildings and simple manufactured objects. Unlike painting packages, this software does not normally allow freehand drawing, instead providing an easy way of drawing straight lines or lines that follow a mathematical curve (such as a circle).

Fig. 8.1 *A GEM Paint display*

Although quite inadequate for professional draughtsmen or architects, drawing software includes several tools found in the more sophisticated computer-aided design packages.

- *Gridlock*, to ensure that the ends of lines are accurately positioned according to a predefined grid of points.
- *Copy*, to reproduce an already-drawn object at other positions in the drawing. So if you are designing an office layout, for example, you can draw one desk and then copy it to a number of locations.
- *Move*, allowing you to re-position an already-drawn object.
- *Delete*, enabling you to remove lines or objects from your drawing.

You can also include a number of standard mathematical objects in your drawing, such as rectangles and circles, and you can add small amounts of text (e.g. captions) to your drawings.

Figure 8.2 shows a screen display from GEM Draw.

Fig. 8.2 *A GEM Draw display*

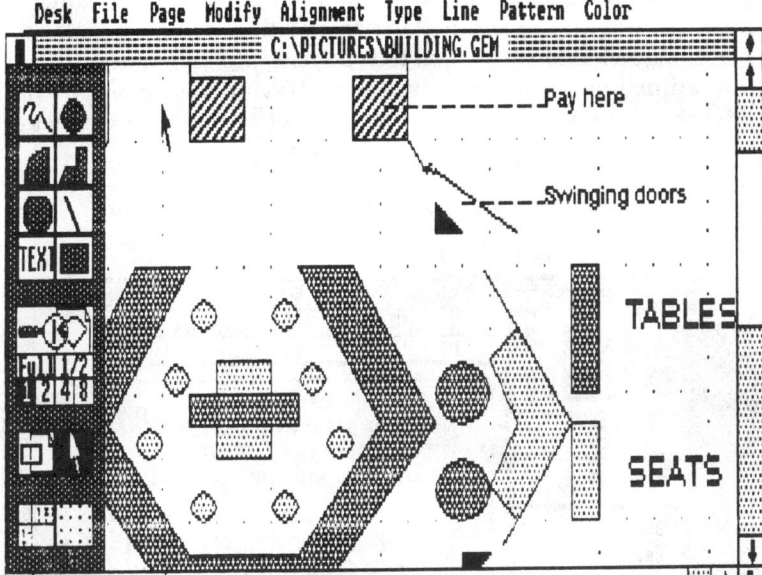

Desk File Page Modify Alignment Type Line Pattern Color

C:\PICTURES\BUILDING.GEM

Pay here

Swinging doors

TABLES

SEATS

c) Wordchart software

Wordchart software enables you to quickly design notices, overhead transparencies, and other single-sheet textual displays. You might think that word processing software would be suitable for this task; however, as explained below, wordcharting software makes the job much easier, and, for the ordinary user, gives a much better result.

Notices and other textual displays can generally be broken down into several *zones*. Typically, these might include:

- a zone in a large typeface, centred, for the title or main heading;
- a multi-line zone in smaller type for a list of topics;
- a further zone, perhaps in italics, to give a date and a venue; and so on.

Wordcharting software provides you with a number of templates, consisting of predefined zones each of which occupies a certain size and generates a certain text font. The layout and sizes of the zones, and the choice of fonts, have been selected by design experts, so you are assured of a good-looking result. This does not restrict you to a few preset designs, however, as you can customise the design – i.e. alter the zone sizes and the fonts – to meet the needs of a particular presentation.

It is a quick and simple job to type text into zones, and to make any adjustments that you require. If you have composed in advance the text of your notice, it takes five minutes or less to produce a wordchart ready for printing.

Fig. 8.3   *A GEM Wordchart display*

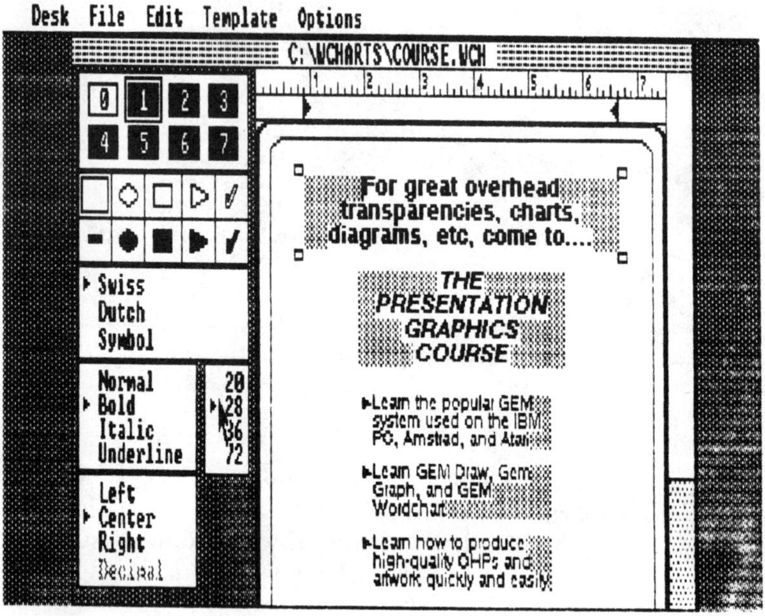

d) Charts and graphs

Presentation graphics packages always include a module to produce high-quality charts and graphs. Normally, a much wider range of charting possibilities are provided than those that are built into a spreadsheet package (see page 89), and sophisticated labelling and titling facilities are provided as well. This type of software allows you to either type in the data, or to read it in from e.g. a Lotus 1-2-3 file.

8.2   Interactive Video

Interactive video systems (IV) allow the viewer to control a video programme using a computer. In practice, this means that the computer and video output appear together on the screen, the computer output often taking the form of either questions on the video sequence just seen, or else a menu of choices for further sequences. The viewer responds by typing at the keyboard, and the computer acts on this to determine which sequences of the video programme are played next.

IV can be achieved by linking a modified home video recorder to a computer. However, videodisc is a much better medium, for reasons which are explained in the next section.

The main application of IV is in education and training. The videodisc in this case will normally contain many short sequences, each one lasting just a few minutes. The video is controlled by computer software in the form of a training package written using special programming language called an *authoring language*. This software carries out the following tasks.

- It dictates the order in which the video sequences are to be played. This can be modified by the learner, either by selecting menu choices or through the way in which he or she responds to questions. A learner with difficulties may be routed by the program through different sequences to a learner that answers the questions correctly.
- It displays questions on the screen to test the learner's understanding of the video sequence just seen.
- It matches the learner's response to a question against a number of possible responses that are stored in the program, and so marks it right or wrong.
- It provides feedback to the user, encouraging him in the case of correct answers and giving explanations in the case of incorrect answers.
- It keeps track of the learner's score for assessment purposes, and of the parts of the course that he or she found difficult.

IV has been found to be a very effective training tool. It has the following advantages over conventional training methods.

- Because the video sequences are interspersed with computer question-and-answer sequences, the learner has to apply his learning at frequent and regular intervals, which helps him retain and understand the material.
- The computer gives immediate feedback when the learner has typed an answer, and provides remedial video instruction in the case of wrong answers. This is highly motivating, as well as ensuring that the learner has understood each point.
- The learner's route through the material can be geared to his needs.

- Because an impersonal machine rather than a human tutor is assessing his work, the learner is less embarrassed and demotivated by wrong answers.
- The material can be presented in a form which is visually attractive and stimulating.

Another major application of IV is point-of-sale (POS). Customers are able to quickly access video sequences on the products that interest them, or find out more about the services offered by a bank or other institution. IV has been successfully used in DHSS offices, where it allows clients to determine their rights and benefits without needing to speak with a DHSS official.

8.3   Videodisc

IV can be based upon videotape or videodisc. The former is relatively low-cost, and can incorporate video material produced fairly cheaply by the training institution itself. However, it has a number of disadvantages compared to the more sophisticated videodisc system described below.

- It takes a long time to wind through the tape to the start of a video sequence, unless that sequence is very close to the previous one.
- It cannot pinpoint sequences in the precise way that is possible with videodisc.
- It cannot pause on a video frame (picture) without distorting the image on the screen and, ultimately, wearing out the tape at that point
- Programming the computer-based material for videotape is time-consuming, owing to the slow search time and the lack of an accurate frame numbering system.

For these reasons, videodisc material is much more suitable for IV.

The main videodisc system used in colleges is Philips Laservision. The Domesday discs from the BBC, for example, are recorded on this system. Other systems are available, however, notably JVC's VHD disk, which is based on electrical capacitance rather than on the optical technology described below. Both types of disc are 30 cm across, the same size as long-playing music records.

Laservision discs store information in the form of tiny pits burned by laser light into the disc's surface. Unlike compact discs, laservision discs work on analogue rather than digital principles: the pits are in fact 'slices' of the waves recorded on them, as shown in Figure 8.4. Both the width of the pits and angles of the edges vary, and on playback these variations are measured by a narrow laser beam which is reflected from them onto the reading head of the laservision player. There is no physical contact between the surface of the disc and the reading head, so Laservision discs are not worn out by repeated playings.

Fig. 8.4   *Pattern of pits on a Laservision disc*

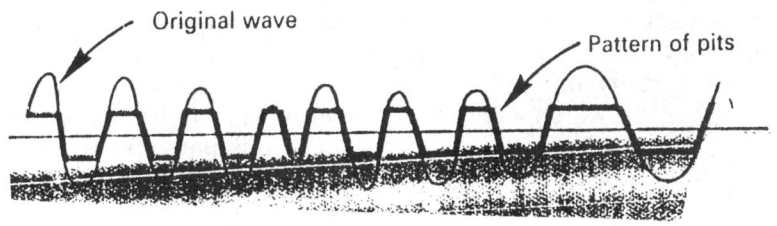

Laservision discs for interactive video are called *active play* discs. Each circular track of an active play disc stores one complete video frame (picture). The player rotates the disc at a constant angular velocity of 25 revolutions per second to play back the video at the standard speed of 25 frames per second.

If you think about this, you will realise that, unlike an ordinary music record, the player must spin the disc faster when it is reading the outer tracks of the disc than when it is reading the inner tracks. This makes for a complex playback mechanism, but it provides the user with a very versatile system:

- If the reading head is held stationary over one rotating track, one frame is reproduced and held on the screen. The reproduction is perfect, unlike the awful picture you get when you try to hold a videotape on a single frame. This means, for example, that you can use a videodisc to store still pictures, such as sets of slides. An active-play disc can store 36 minutes of video per side, and since each second of video playback uses 25 frames, it is easy to work out the number of still pictures that can be stored on one side of a disc:

$$36 \times 60 \times 25 = 54\,000 \text{ pictures}$$

- Each frame can be identified by a number, and the player can access any frame simply by moving the reading head to the corresponding track. Any frame from the 54 000 stored on a side of a disc can be accessed in under two seconds. It is this numbering system that is used by the associated computer software to control the videoplayer.

To make a videodisc, the video sequences must first be shot using the professional C-format video system. When the final tape is edited and ready, a videodisc master is produced from it using a laser light process, and the individual discs are pressed from this.

The production of the video film is the most expensive part of the process, though other elements, such as writing the associated computer program, are not cheap. The total cost of producing an interactive videodisc, with the software, is likely to exceed £100 000. As a result, IV training packages are expensive, often several hundred pounds per copy – which is why there are not too many of them around in colleges. Nevertheless, IV packages are widely used in a number of big companies, where the large numbers who use them make this powerful training medium a cost-effective tool.

8.4   Compact Discs

Compact discs are now widely used for music recordings. They store information in a digital form, which means that, unlike ordinary analogue recordings, there is no degradation of the signal. If the reproduction is less than perfect, then the fault lies with the other analogue parts of the system – such as the microphones and the loudspeakers – rather than the compact discs themselves.

Being digital, compact discs clearly have an important role in the digital world of IT. For besides audio recordings, they can be used to store computer data and text, as well as video images in digital form.

Laser light represents a binary 1 by a short pulse of light from a laser gun, and a binary 0 by the absence of a pulse. To store information on a compact disc, very powerful pulses are used, which burn tiny pits in its surface. As the disc rotates, and the laser gun works its way like a gramophone stylus across the surface, a tightly-packed spiral of tracks consisting of thousands of tiny pits is built up.

On playback, the process works in reverse. A low-powered laser beam scans the tracks of the rotating disc, being reflected back by the silvered surface. The pits on the surface are ¼ of the wavelength of the laser light in depth, so light reflected from the bottom of a pit is exactly out of phase with light relected from the surface. It therefore interferes with it, largely cancelling it out. The returning beam strikes a photoelectric cell, which converts the light to electrical pulses. The less intense light from a pit produces a smaller pulse than light reflected from a spot on the surface which doesn't contain a pit. In this way the original pattern of 1s and 0s is reproduced.

As with videodisc, there is no physical contact between the surface of the disc and the playback mechanism, and so no wear is caused by repeated playings, and grease or dust normally has no effect. Unlike videodisc, a compact disc is only 5.25″ across, the same as an ordinary floppy disk.

8.5 Compact Discs for Data Storage

The great advantage of magnetic storage media such as floppy disks is the ease with which old information can be erased from them and replaced by new. Magnetic media have several disadvantages, though:

● the information recorded on them can become corrupted if the disk is stored in a magnetic field, or if its surface gets dirty;
● a relatively small amount of information only can be stored on floppy disk; floppy disks are certainly adequate for ordinary office applications, but when it comes to multimedia computing, for example, a floppy disk will only hold a handful of digitised pictures.

Hence the interest in compact discs for storing computer data. Compact discs are very robust, and a single disc can store several hundred Mbytes of data. Used in this role, a compact disc is called a *CD-ROM*, short for 'Compact Disc – Read-Only Memory'. It has this name because an ordinary compact disc cannot be written to (i.e. recorded on), only read.

A typical CD-ROM application is storing large databases, which can then be sent through the post to client offices and firms. Details of all university courses, for example, are stored in this way, and sent to educational clients. These discs will, of course, become out of date, and so update information may be sent out at regular intervals on floppy disk or over the phone line.

CD-ROMs are read using a CD-ROM drive, which is about the

same size as an ordinary floppy disk drive and which costs a few hundred pounds. The CD-ROMs themselves, of course, have to be mastered from the original magnetic storage media and copies pressed. A number of organisations exist that undertake this type of work.

Another type of compact disc is the WORM disc, short for 'Write Once Read Many times'. A WORM drive costs around £2000, but it is able to write data to a blank compact disc as well as read from it. It cannot, though, erase and overwrite data that has already been recorded. A typical application is archiving files to a compact disc, where the lack of an erase facility is a positive advantage. This is not only safer than archiving them to floppy disks (which can be erased and which are not very robust), it makes retrieval much easier as a huge number of files can be stored on the one disk.

New types of compact disc are being developed which, like floppies, can be erased. These should be commercially available within a few years. When they arrive, they will no doubt have a major impact on computer storage, especially for large databases and for multimedia applications.

8.6   Compact Disc for Multimedia Applications

The huge capacity of compact discs means that they can store large amounts of computer data, text, images, and sound. Encyclopaedias, for example, are now being published in compact disc form. This not only makes them very compact, it also means that, since they can be linked to the power of the computer, all entries on a selected topic can be rapidly retrieved and displayed on the screen.

Another development is *CD-V*, short for 'Compact Disc – Video', which will be used for high-quality sound and video. One obvious application for CD-V is pop videos.

There are also interesting possibilities of computer-controlled multi-media presentations using compact disc systems. These could form a low-cost alternative to IV systems. Philips, for example, is working on *CD-I*, which stands for 'Compact Disc – Interactive', and hopes to bring out a CD-I player by the end of the 80s. This will cost a fraction of the price of a videodisc player, and will use comparatively inexpensive compact discs.

CD-I aims to take full advantage of the enormous capacity of compact discs for storing images and sounds as well as text, and combine this with the power of the computer to develop a new publishing medium. This will revolutionise encyclopaedias, dictionaries, training materials, and so on, which ideally contain visual, aural, and textual components. A single disc is able to hold a complete English-language dictionary, including the words in audio and some accompanying pictures in (still) video.

Like interactive video, the computer software will allow the user to access any part of the disc by means of a system of menus or questions, and if necessary will conduct him through the disc as part of a training package, with questions, feedback, and branching.

Unlike interactive video, the pictures are digitised, and have to be read from the disc and processed by the computer before they can be displayed on the screen. The quality is high, and each picture occupies about 100 Kbytes of screen memory. The disc-access speed is around 150 Kbytes per second, so the time to access and display one full picture is between two and three seconds. So true moving pictures are impossible with this system.

However, if reduced-size pictures are displayed, occupying, say, only ⅙ of the screen, then that time reduces to ¹⁄₁₀ second, which means that reasonably good animation is possible. Typically, the animated sequence will appear in a fairly small window on the screen, and text or computer graphics will appear alongside it.

The Philips machine will have two video processors, which means that it can display simultaneously two different signals from the disc, e.g. text and real pictures. So it can be used in much the same way as interactive video, at a fraction of the (hardware) price.

8.7 Multimedia Computing and the Arts

During the past half-century, information technology, in its widest sense, has revolutionised the media, bringing into being radio, cinema, TV, records, and audio and video cassettes. Each of these has had an enormous and obvious impact on the arts. Today, the main thrust of IT is centred on computers, and developments in multimedia computing are having a major impact on artistic productions of all kinds.

It is influencing the arts in two ways.

- It increases the tools available to the artist, so offering a new range of possibilities. Electronic music is one example.
- It increases the productivity of the artist, enabling him to produce more. One example is provided by computer animation techniques, which allow the artist to create a

sequence by drawing a small number of key frames. From these the computer is able to work out and produce the intermediate frames needed to achieve the animated effect.

Computers are now being applied to all the major forms of art. Here are some examples.

- *Music* – Hardware and software for the production of synthesised music and for enhancing music produced in traditional ways are now an established part of the recording scene. Features provided by these systems include a wide range of musical sounds and effects, and the ability to alter, throughout a composition, variables such as pitch, tempo, and loudness. Another feature incorporated in some systems is the automatic generation and printing of sheet music for works composed directly on the keyboard.
- *Animation and visual effects* – Computer animation, which made possible a number of films such as the *Star Wars* series, is now becoming an art form in its own right. A number of short films made entirely by computer have now been released. Computer graphics, video titling, and other computer-based techniques are also widely used in TV production.
- *Writing* – Writers can now obtain computer software which will express their prose in crisp, simple English. You can, for example, process paragraphs taken from the works of Dickens with this software, with remarkably effective results. It does not make such good literature, but it is certainly simpler to read and understand.
- *Games* – The computer game, especially the adventure game, is becoming a quite new form of art. The more sophisticated games incorporate impressive computer graphics, and the quality of the synthesised music that is used with some of them can also be impressive.

Assignment 5

Imagine you are a student in your college in the year 2010. Multimedia instructional materials are now widely used, and, with the enormous growth in satellite communications, it is not even necessary for the college to have this available in its own library. Statistical data and other information for research projects is also readily available over communications links.

Describe your college work during the course of one day in that year. You will need to think about how these hi-tech systems will affect your timetable (will there be a fixed timetable, even?), and your learning experiences in individual subjects. You should also think about how your assignments will be assessed in this kind of environment, and how this will affect the way you produce them.

Conclude your account with an appraisal of the advantages and disadvantages of studying in 2010 compared with studying today.

Questions

1 Write down three applications of a presentation graphics package in a college office.
2 Interactive video is claimed to be more effective than any other training medium. Summarise the reasons for this.
3 Give three reasons why compact discs are important for the future of IT and computing.
4 Give three advantages of publishing reference works such as encyclopaedias in compact disc form.

Chapter 9
The Second Industrial Revolution

The cottage industries of two or three centuries ago were engaged in the small-scale production of individually-crafted products. Automated production methods were unknown, and most jobs were one-offs or produced in small batches.

All this changed with the Industrial Revolution, which created large-scale production units with a vast output of manufactured goods. This led, on the one hand, to the enormous material prosperity of the industrialised world. On the other hand, however, it led to the demise of individually-made products which could be customised to suit different tastes. As was said of the early cars that rolled off the Ford production lines, 'You can have any colour, so long as it's black'.

Today, manufacturing enterprises are able to combine the economies of large-scale production with cottage-industry's flexibility of being able to produce individual or small batches of customised goods. This is called *flexible manufacturing*, and it is one of the components of a second industrial revolution which is now underway, based upon the silicon chip. Other components of this revolution are computer-aided design and the integrated factory.

This chapter deals with this second industrial revolution. Chapter 10 explains how this aspect of the information revolution may change our lives, both as producers and consumers.

9.1 The Production Process

We can list the stages in the production process that takes place in a manufacturing business as follows.

- The first stage is to design products that the business is able to produce and that people will want to buy. Assessing consumer demand is normally carried out by the market research function in the business, and may use data drawn from market surveys. Design is a continuing and evolving process: consumer wants and preferences change over time, and technological change can also affect design.

- The next stage is to draw up the production plans for the period ahead. This will be based upon the numbers of orders that are anticipated and received, as well as the need to maintain stocks of goods. Again, this is a continuing process: plans have to be drawn up for the next period as this approaches, and any new products or design changes to existing products have to be incorporated in it. Two key terms used in production planning are *scheduling* and *loading*. The former means the task of deciding when jobs are to be done, the latter means deciding which work groups and machines are to do them.
- The next stage is to use the raw materials or parts received from suppliers to produce the goods.
- The final stage is to distribute the goods to dealers, customers, or the finished-goods store.

Let's see how these stages of the production process are being affected by the silicon chip.

9.2 Data Processing

We'll begin with the system that lies at the back of a number of these stages, namely the data processing (DP) system. This is used for many tasks, including:

- processing customers' orders to produce not only the sales documentation but also to calculate the quantities to be made and supplied during the coming period;
- processing goods-received and goods-issued data to maintain the stock records and to contribute to the calculations of quantities to be produced;
- processing market research and other information from outside the firm to help decide on product evolution and to contribute to the calculations of quantities to be produced;
- carrying out calculations to help determine what the production plans for the coming period should be, based on the above results;
- calculating from these production plans the quantities of raw materials and parts needed to be bought in or made, and producing the necessary purchase orders and other documentation.

Data processing is, of course, almost invariably done today by computer, and the first impact that the IT revolution had on the factory was in this area. It speeded up the 'paperwork' greatly, cut out errors, and resulted in vastly improved production plans, lower stock levels, and improved cash flow.

It's worth noting that in a large computer system, such as the kind of mainframe system that is often used for data processing in a large manufacturing business, all the above processing will be *integrated*. In an integrated DP system, the various files – stock records, customer records, and so on – can be accessed by any part of the system. This enables the computer to bring together all the information needed, for example, to help calculate the production plans.

9.3   Computer-aided Design

A computer-aided design (CAD) package uses the power of the computer to do for drawings what a word processing package does for text. It was the second main way in which IT revolutionised the production process.

Like WP, CAD enables you to:

- delete, insert, copy, and move things rapidly and easily around on the computer screen;
- insert existing material stored on disk – such as drawings of parts and sub-assemblies – into your latest masterpiece, so that you are not constantly reinventing (or rather re-drawing) the wheel;
- format your work, so that it is printed or plotted in the colours, line types and so on, that you require.

CAD packages also offer a number of additional and valuable drawing aids:

- the computer's equivalent of geometric tools such as the compass, the ruler, the protractor, and arcs;
- the computer's equivalent of the nib, that allows you to draw different types and thicknesses of lines;
- a grid, so that the start and end points of any lines that you draw are locked onto a grid of 'graph paper' points on the screen;
- zoom facilities, enabling you to expand any part of your drawing on the screen and thereby work more accurately;
- rotating, inverting, and other facilities enabling you to manipulate parts of your drawing in a very flexible way;

- scaling facilities, enabling you to type in line lengths, angles, and other dimensions at the keyboard, the computer converting these to the required lines on the screen;
- dimensioning facilities, which automatically calculate and display on your drawing the lengths of any lines that you may have drawn.

The keyboard is not a suitable drawing tool, and so CAD systems normally use a mouse or similar device.

CAD systems can achieve impressive productivity gains in drawing offices, and it is often claimed that a 400% increase in output can be achieved. This does, however, assume that the draughtsman is familiar with the CAD system and is using its capabilities to the full.

To give an example of the speed at which an item can be drawn, consider a spoked wheel. To draw this, it is only necessary to draw a single spoke and then rotate it through 360 degrees about the centre point of the wheel, duplicating the spoke say every 15 degrees. The hub and the rim can then be rapidly drawn using the CAD package's electronic compass. Any bolts or other parts can be called up from a library held on disk and inserted as required on the drawing.

Even greater productivity can be achieved when the CAD system is linked directly to the CAM system, described below. Then, the CAD data can be used directly to control the settings of automatic machines in the factory.

9.4 Computer-aided Manufacture

Computer-aided manufacture (CAM) refers to the use of computers to control the manufacturing process, primarily by controlling the settings of tools and the way they are used in computer-numerically-controlled (CNC) machines and other automatic devices, and by controlling the deployment of industrial robots. The CAM system uses the production plans produced by the DP system, and the product designs produced by the CAD system, to work out what should be made at what times and on which machines.

To understand what's involved, you should know that factory production typically involves two major processes:

- the machining of parts;
- the handling of parts and their assembly.

Today, CNC machines can carry out the first process very efficiently, even for small runs. Operating automatically under software instructions, they can apply various drilling, turning, and cutting devices to the raw material to produce an accurately-made part.

Robots can carry out the second of these processes, for they can handle materials and feed them to the CNC machines. They can also remove the finished parts and, if necessary, assemble them to make the finished products. Like CNC machines, they can be used economically for small runs. An industrial robot typically consists of a robot arm with a clasping device or other tools attached.

Early generations of CNC machines and robots lacked 'intelligence', meaning that they did not have sensory devices enabling them to respond to changes in their environment. In the case of robots, this meant that they would perform the sequence of operations dictated by the controlling software, blindly picking up and manipulating whatever object happened to be placed in the operating position, or, if nothing was there, picking up and manipulating empty space.

Modern generations of CNC machines and robots are equipped with sensors enabling them to identify and locate objects, and so make adjustments to the programmed sequence of operations that they have to perform. In essence, a machine of this type consists of three systems.

- A mechanical system to operate tools or to pick up and manipulate objects. This system may include rotating shafts, drills, and other tools, as well as clasping and other handling devices.
- A sensory system to detect what the mechanical system is doing and, in the case of robots, to identify and locate objects. A variety of sensing devices are used, including, for robots, video 'eyes'.
- A control system which interprets the information received by the sensory system and uses it to control the mechanical system. This system is normally based on silicon chips.

In simple terms, the sequence of operations that takes place when one of these machines performs a task is as follows.

- The sensory system converts the position of a part into an electrical signal.
- The control system compares this with an ideal computed position based on data from the controlling program.

- The difference between the two is the 'error', and it is represented by minute digital pulses of electricity.
- These pulses are fed to the mechanical system, where they are converted to analogue form, and amplified to the level needed to adjust the positions of the arms and tools.

In a CAM system, a production line consists of CNC machines, robot arms, and materials transfer systems, all under the control of a central computer.

9.5 Flexible Manufacturing Systems

Because modern CNC machines and robots are software-driven, they can be switched from task to task in a very flexible way. Also, production plans can be equally flexible, because they are calculated by the computer data processing system. The result is *flexible manufacturing systems* (FMS), a term used to describe the ability of modern manufacturing operations to switch rapidly from one product specification to another.

FMS offers great benefits for many types of production.

- Batch production, which accounts for a large part of the manufacturing activity of an industrialised country, can be automated, with resulting cost and quality benefits.
- Large scale production is no longer tied to huge production runs of identical products. A car manufacturing plant, for example, can make cars to order without incurring heavy set-up costs. This means that dealers or customers can specify the colours and accessories required, and the quantities, and these can be quickly assembled.
- The factory can operate on a *just in time* (JIT) basis, as products can be made to order at the time that they are required, rather than being made for stock weeks or months in advance. This cuts down greatly on stock-holding costs.

9.6 The Integrated Factory

The DP system, the CAD system, and the CAM system can be closely tied together by electronic links, or *integrated*. There must be a large computer (typically a mainframe) in overall control of these systems, running special software such as the TIME software described in the next section. This same computer may also run the DP system and the CAD system, in which case the links between these systems will be purely software links.

The first phase in this integration is to link the CAD system to the CAM system, to create a *CAD/CAM* system. In this, the product design created on the CAD software is converted by the CAM software to instructions for the factory machines, so that the settings for the machines and the tools used are automatically determined.

In the second phase, the DP system is tied to the CAD/CAM system to create what's sometimes called an *integrated factory*. In this, the information from customers' orders is used to control the scheduling and loading of work in the factory, so that it automatically produces what's required. As well as this, the DP system is linked to the CAD system, so that it passes to it management reports and market information for use in product design.

These key systems that make up the integrated factory are shown in Figure 9.1. Note that the links that are shown in the diagram between these systems take place via the controlling software, as explained in the next section.

At present, CAD/CAM is quite widely employed, but few integrated factories exist, apart from some in Japan.

Fig. 9　*The key systems in an integrated factory*

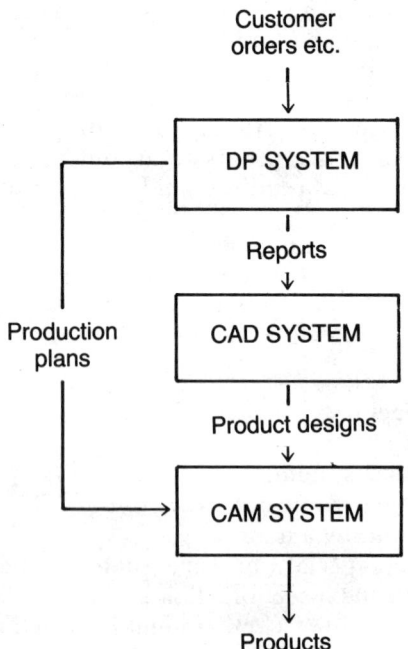

9.7 Controlling the Integrated Factory

One example of software for controlling the integrated factory is *TIME*, short for Tandem Integrated Manufacturing Environment. As its name implies, this system is a product of Tandem Computers, and runs on their mainframes.

A schematic of the TIME system is shown in Figure 9.2. It consists of three modules, called *Factory Manager*, *Document Manager*, and *Device Manager*. These modules perform the following broad tasks.

- The Factory Manager controls the minute-by-minute progress of parts through the factory, to ensure that orders are produced at the right time and to the right specifications. The basis of this control is information on customer orders obtained from the DP system.
- The Document Manager takes the designs produced by the CAD system and passes them around the factory to the machines that require them, when they require them.
- The Device Manager is really the interface between these two managers and the factory machines. It interprets the information produced by the Factory Manager and the Document Manager into the instructions that are passed to the CNC machines, robots, and other factory devices.

Fig. 9.2 *Schematic of the TIME system*

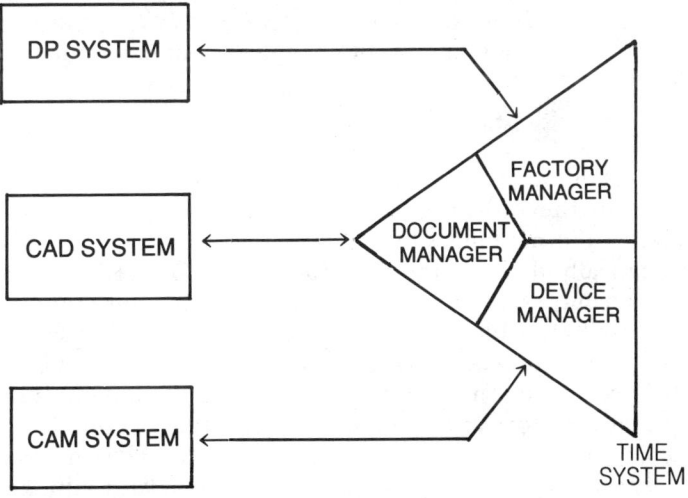

9.8 The Impact of IT on Commerce

The IT revolution is also having a major impact on the related world of commerce. This includes the distribution, marketing, and retailing of manufactured products, and the provision of ancillary services such as banking and finance. This section reviews some of the developments that are taking place in these areas.

a) Retailing and banking
IT is changing not only existing retailing and banking practices, but introducing some quite new ones. Broadly speaking, these changes are as follows.

- The development of cashless shopping, using Visa, Access, and similar cards.

- The development of advanced point-of-sale terminals, able to identify bar-coded goods and so automatically produce the customer's bill using price information stored in the system. These systems can also send electronically the sales details to the stock control system, which in turn is able to automatically activate the ordering procedures.

- The introduction of electronic shopping, via Prestel and other on-line systems.

- The introduction of home banking and other financial services on Prestel and other networks, so that bills can be paid and other transactions enacted at any time via a computer.

Other developments that are starting to make their appearance include further advances in point-of-sale terminals which are linked to the banking system, so that customers' accounts are automatically debited and the store's account credited. At our local Sainsbury's, for example, I can even draw out money from their terminals, which then automatically debit my bank account.

The so-called *smart card* is another important development. This looks like an ordinary plastic card, but it contains a silicon chip that can store and calculate the details of all purchases for which it is used. These details are periodically read from the card by a special machine in the customer's bank, and adjustments made to his or her account.

b) Computer trading

Another example of the impact of IT on commerce is the use of the computer for stock market trading. Before 1986 the floor of the Stock Exchange in London was crammed with traders in stocks and shares, buying and selling on behalf of clients. This all disappeared with the installation of computers able to trade with other similar computers not only in London but also in other stock markets around the world.

Not only can these computers buy and sell electronically in response to instructions entered at the keyboard, they can also carry out automatic trading without any human intervention. This is called *programmed trading*, and it works by monitoring movements in stocks and shares, buying when prices move significantly upwards and selling when prices are moving down.

Unfortunately, this is not quite as clever as it sounds, for it was programmed trading that caused much of the massive selling that took place in the global stock market on 'Black Monday' in October 1987. Once prices started to slide, the computers took over with their programmed selling and forced further falls. If this had been allowed to continue, most shares would have been wiped out completely, causing the total collapse of the world's financial markets. So programmed trading was turned off, leaving people in charge, and the slide in prices was checked.

It's one example of the dangers of allowing computers to make important decisions.

c) Expert systems

An expert system is a type of software package that is being increasingly used in commerce and industry, as well as in other fields such as medicine. What an expert system does is store the knowledge of experts in a particular subject or *domain* in what's called a *knowledge base*. This knowledge is organised in the form of *facts* and *rules*. The experts are interviewed at terminals by the *knowledge engineers* who build this kind of system, and the facts and rules that are elicited from them are linked together in the knowledge base.

Expert systems can be of considerable value:

- because a number of experts are normally involved in constructing them, the amount of knowledge they contain is greater than the knowledge of any one human expert;

- the power of the computer means that links can be built between facts and rules which were not apparent before, so improving the quality of the knowledge;

● once constructed, they can be supplied to many users, making the precious expertise widely available to people who are not themselves expert in the domain.

To retrieve knowledge from a knowledge base, the user enters at a keyboard the question that he or she wants answered. The computer will then respond by requesting further information, and after further questions and answers which enable the computer to get all the relevant facts, the answer to the original question is given. Sometimes, a definitive answer may not be possible, as in the case of a medical diagnosis, in which case the computer may give two or three possible answers, assigning probabilities to each.

The software used to store, organise, and interrogate a knowledge base is called an expert system *shell*. Many of these shells run on mainframe and minicomputers, though a number are available on personal computers. Like database software, an expert system shell can be used for a variety of applications, ranging from the repair of a particular make of helicopter to providing advice on DHSS regulations.

Expert systems have now been developed for a large number of domains, including aspects of medicine, geology, mathematics, law, business, and repair and maintenance of equipment.

One example of an expert system for commerce is Sales Edge, a package produced by the Human Edge Software Corporation for the Apple Macintosh. This can be used to analyse the personality factors of the parties involved in a transaction (the seller and the buyer), from which it advises the salesman on the strategy to adopt. When the salesman runs the program, he is asked to agree or disagree with a number of statements about himself, and then to agree or disagree with a number of adjectives that describe the buyer. When this has been done, the program produces a sales strategy in the form of a report several pages long.

Questions

1 Why can the introduction of DP into a manufacturing business result in lower stock levels and improved cash flow?
2 Give three reasons why CAD can improve productivity in a drawing office by up to 400%.

3 Many jobs can be computerised or robotised, but hairdressing isn't one of them. Why do you think this is?

4 FMS benefits both the manufacturer and the customer. Give one benefit for the manufacturer, and one for the customer.

5 Write down two benefits to the retailer of bar coding.

6 One application of expert systems is repair and maintenance. What advantages over manuals do these have for the repairman?

Chapter 10

IT and the Individual

IT is having an increasing impact on every part of our lives. At work, it is changing the content of jobs. Old skills and practices are disappearing, and new ones emerging. New machines and new products are developed at an ever-increasing rate, creating new opportunities and new jobs, while companies and industries that stick with old technology decline, shedding jobs.

In the home, the silicon chip is used in more and more appliances. We read of the 'intelligent home', in which the central heating system, the burglar alarm, the video, and other systems are all controlled by a central computer. Our leisure has been radically altered by that all-pervasive product of the IT age, TV. In the field of education and training, computer-based training is steadily encroaching upon traditional methods. Further examples of the way IT affects us as individuals include police surveillance technology, and the use of computers by government agencies to store personal data.

So how is IT going to affect you, as you set out on your life as an employee, as a consumer, and as a citizen? This final chapter deals with this important aspect of the information revolution.

10.1 IT and the Employee

All technological revolutions, from the Stone Age on, have transformed both the content of jobs and the pattern of employment. What sets the IT revolution apart from the rest is the sheer speed with which the changes are taking place.

When I started my working life, the only computers were mainframes, and most of those were used for scientific and engineering work. IT as a concept and a subject discipline was almost unknown. Today, I am still far from retirement, and it seems that in those few short years IT has permeated every aspect of work. Almost everyone's job is greatly affected in some way or other by the computer.

This section examines firstly the way in which IT has affected what jobs there are available, and secondly how it affects the nature of those jobs.

a) Employment levels
Look at Figure 10.1. It charts the relationship between the number of employees and the industrial output of developed countries for the period 1950 to 1980.

- Between 1950 and 1965, employment and output both increased, as shown by the first upward-sloping section of the graph. These increases were due to the new factories and plants being set up at this time to take advantage of the latest manufacturing technology.
- From 1965 to 1973, output grew rapidly while employment remained static, as shown by the second flat section of the graph. At this time, the manufacturing technology matured, and the increase in output was achieved by productivity improvements and by making plants more efficient.
- From 1973 to 1980, there was a slight increase in output, but a significant decrease in employment. At this time, many markets became saturated, and competition between firms increased. This resulted in further improvements in productivity by successful firms, while other factories were forced to close down.

Fig. 10.1 *Relationship between employment and output, 1950 to 1980*

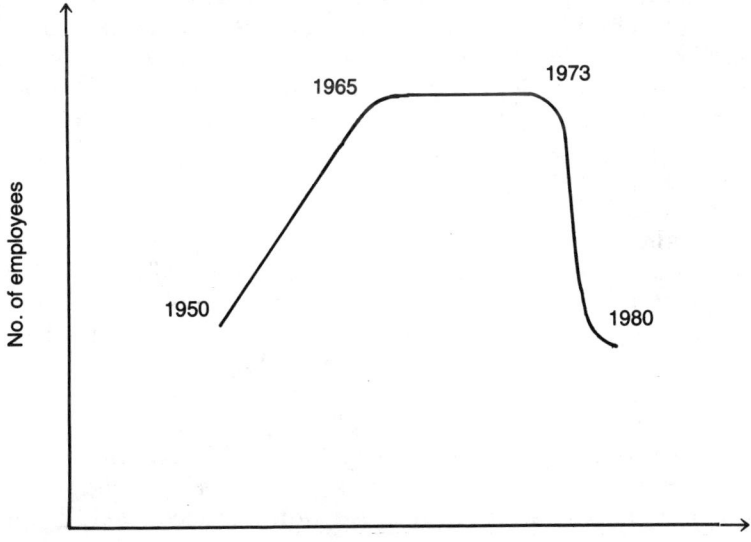

This graph, it seems, is one segment of a wave-like cycle that has been going on ever since the Industrial Revolution began:

- every 50 or so years there is an upswing in the employment/output ratio, caused by the introduction of a new technological style;
- this is followed by a flattening in employment as the technology matures;
- then comes a shake-out in employment as competition becomes more intense.

The existence of these waves was discovered in 1935 by Kondratieff, and so they are called *Kondratieff* waves.

The last upswing started after the depression of the thirties. Today, some 50 years on, we appear to be at the start of a new upswing. The technological style underlying this upswing is the silicon chip, which is starting to be introduced into manufacturing processes. Robots and other computer-controlled machines are appearing, and computer-controlled 'integrated' factories – described in the last chapter – are being planned.

If history repeats itself, we can expect to see a significant increase in both output and employment over the next 20 years or so as these new kinds of machines and new kinds of factories are constructed. This will be followed by a period of static or declining employment, as the technology matures and competition sets in.

Whether or not we will see such a rerun of history remains to be seen. This much is clear, however, from the experience of the last two centuries: it is a gross over-simplification to assume that developing technology and automatic equipment can only lead to a reduction in jobs. It does lead to a reduction at the end of the technological cycle; at the beginning, though, it leads to increased employment.

In the UK, the regions which have the lowest unemployment and the highest wage rates are those which have implemented the new technology to the greatest extent. In the industrialised world as a whole, it is significant that concern about unemployment is being replaced by concern about the lack of trained labour to fill the jobs that are being created by the new technologies.

b) Job content
If there are going to be plenty of jobs available over the next two decades, what sort of jobs are they going to be? Many claim that IT will de-skill and dehumanise work; indeed, we all know

people who do not like working with computers, because they spend most of their day keying in figures.

However, like the employment issue, the job content issue is not that simple. For computers can also make jobs more interesting, by taking away the boring parts and allowing the worker to undertake a wider range of tasks. My own job is an example of this (see page 2).

A key factor seems to be the way in which management implements the new technology. There are two possible approaches.

- There is the *production-line* approach, in which tasks are split into small elements, and each worker undertakes just one or two of those elements. This is a very efficient way of organising work, as people do not spend time moving from one task to another, and the training needed is minimal. However, under this system, jobs can be very monotonous, people tend to become alienated from their work, and morale is low.
- There is the *whole-task* approach, in which each worker undertakes every part of a task. This may not be as technically efficient as the production-line approach, and it requires more training. However, it gives the worker a more stimulating and fulfilling job, which improves morale and can increase productivity.

As an example of these two alternative approaches, consider the work of typists and word processor operators. In one firm, a typist/operator may spend all day at the keyboard, while other office jobs such as filing the correspondence are done by other clerks (who never get to touch a keyboard). In another firm, the jobs of typists and clerks may be combined, so that each worker undertakes a full range of duties. Normally, this will be organised so that each person deals with all the typing and clerical work generated by one group of executives, so seeing each task through from its inception to its completion.

Automatic equipment, such as the computer, accentuates the effects of these two approaches. If tasks are broken down on a production-line basis, the computer will reduce the range of operations that have to be performed still further. If the whole-task approach is adopted, the computer, by automating the mindless parts of the task, can have the effect of giving the individual more time and therefore the potential to increase his or her range of responsibilities.

So the computer has the effect of exaggerating tendencies,

already present in the work situation, to either dehumanise or to enhance jobs. The key factor is management's attitudes to jobs and job design rather than the technology that is employed. If management has an enlightened attitude to job design, then computers and related equipment such as robots can be a boon. They can cut out the boring parts of jobs, and, in the case of robots, they can reduce the exposure of workers to hostile and dangerous environments.

c) Employment patterns

During recent centuries, and especially since the Industrial Revolution, there has been a steady shift in employment away from the primary sector of industrialised economies into the secondary and tertiary sectors. (The primary sector is to do with the extraction of raw materials and the production of food; the secondary sector covers manufacturing; and the tertiary sector refers to service industries such as banking, insurance, marketing, and retailing.)

A few centuries ago, most of the labour force worked on the land (primary sector). Today, only one or two per cent are employed in this way. A few decades ago, most people were employed in manufacturing (secondary sector). Today, in mature economies such as those of the Western nations, the majority work in the tertiary sector.

With the increasing computerisation and robotisation of manufacturing, these trends will continue. In two decades from now, manufacturing employment might drop to the kinds of levels that we associate with farming. If this is the case, then 95% of the workforce will be employed in jobs in the service industries, or in the 'office' side of manufacturing.

Most people will then be 'information' workers. Advances in computing and telecommunications will therefore greatly affect their jobs. We see today the beginning of a trend for these people to work at home, with information passing between their computers and others via the phone lines. In some measure, perhaps, we are returning to the cottage industry ways of working that characterised life before the Industrial Revolution.

How far this trend will go remains to be seen, as it cuts out much of the social contact that is so important at work. Nevertheless, the evolution of computing and telecommunications is encouraging the decentralisation of office and administrative activities. In the UK this is one factor that may bring about a shift of work away from the high-cost Southeast to other parts of the country.

10.2   IT and the Consumer

IT has had a major and obvious impact on the consumer. TVs, videos, the telephone, and home computers, are all products of the IT age, and most modern domestic appliances include a chip-based control mechanism. IT has not only greatly increased the range of products that are available, it has made those products widely available at a low price. By the standards of a mere 20 years ago, today's videos, TVs, and other electronic consumer products are not only amazingly sophisticated, they are also remarkably cheap.

This section of the chapter examines the key trends in IT for you as a consumer, and looks at some of the key products and services that are now emerging.

a) Education and training
Education and training are, in the final analysis, consumer products, developed and marketed like any other consumer products. They are becoming increasingly important as new skills are demanded by the new industries and old skills disappear. Traditional ways of imparting these skills, such as day-release courses at colleges, are not the whole answer to this need, and are in any case suited to only a minority of people. More flexible learning methods, based upon the application of new technology, are coming into vogue.

There is a great deal of emphasis now on 'open' learning, i.e. learning which is not dependent upon travelling to a college at fixed times. Courses are available which can be done in the learner's own time and in his own home. These may be based upon books and traditional learning materials; increasingly, though, they are making use of new technology. Some indication of the changes that are taking place was given earlier in this book. Multimedia computer-based learning materials, and delivery systems based upon broadband telecommunications links, are two key trends.

The benefits that can result from the application of new technology to education and training have encouraged the production of significant amounts of computer-based open learning material. The EEC itself is embarking on an ambitious project, called *Delta*, to make high-technology open learning materials available in the 1990s in a range of languages across the Community. Many of these materials will employ a range of media, including computer graphics, digitised video material, and audio.

The Delta project will involve transmitting these materials by satellite and other means. The target audience will be adult learners all over the EEC, who should be able to pick up transmissions by cable or dish in their homes, offices, or at special centres. The project also assumes that they will have access to powerful but low-cost learner 'stations', i.e. personal computers with advanced multimedia capabilities, able to handle the kind of learning materials that are envisaged.

Because of the size of the target audience, the cost per student-hour of these materials is likely to be very low. This means that it will be feasible to produce and transmit a wide range of educational and training materials for the unemployed and for people with special educational needs, as well as for people in employment needing to learn new skills.

b) The home

Sophisticated domestic appliances controlled by the silicon chip have been with us for many years now. We can expect further levels of sophistication in the future, with significant reductions in cost as more automated production methods become established. Quite new products, such as CD-Video players, will also come onto the market.

We can also see emerging a trend towards common interfaces between these various devices. To give one example, many home computers can be linked to TV sets and videos. A great deal of effort is currently being expended in this direction, and the European Commission has awarded £2.5 million to a group of companies led by Thorn-EMI to develop the necessary communications standards. These standards, when designed and implemented, will mean that all the devices that conform to them will work together.

The final goal of this effort is the emergence of *integrated home systems*, or IHS for short. In an integrated home, all the appliances, from the burglar alarm to the central heating system, will be linked together and controlled by a central computer. Thorn-EMI has already built a prototype house embodying these principles.

This is the kind of scenario envisaged for a family living in such a house:

Returning home from a family outing, you are delayed by a motorway accident. The house is empty and in darkness, with the curtains open, an attractive target for burglars. Your meal, which is in the oven set to cook on automatic, will be cold by the time you arrive. The central heating timer will switch on the heating unnecessarily early. You will miss the final episode of the TV serial you have been watching.

Your home and its appliances are, however, under the control of your computerised IHS. By phoning home, you can access this system. This means that you can reprogram the oven, reset the central heating system, set the video recorder, close the curtains, check that the burglar alarm system is on, and switch on the lights in a predetermined sequence to simulate people at home.

Far-fetched? Pocket calculators were far-fetched when I was at college, and personal computers were beyond one's wildest dreams.

c) Shopping and banking

The impact of IT on shopping and banking was examined on page 146 At one time, it was predicted that the day would come when most shopping and banking transactions would be carried out electronically from home, via Prestel and similar services. Although a small amount is done this way, there is no indication that electronic methods will displace traditional shops and banks. Instead, the main impact of IT is to enhance conventional services.

In the case of shopping, this means the continued development of point-of-sale, payment, and ordering systems, so that ever-larger stores can be managed efficiently. This benefits the customer by providing a very wide range of goods under a single roof. Point-of-sale terminals can now be linked to the banking system, so avoiding the need for cash or credit-card payments: customers' bank accounts can be automatically debited and the store's account credited.

This, and the use of the smart card (page 146), means that we will become more of a cashless society, transferring funds electronically rather than by means of coins, paper money, and cheques.

10.3   IT and the Citizen

This section examines the impact of IT on your life as a citizen. The main thrust of IT here is in the area of public control, where there are two key developments.

- The establishment of computerised databases by a variety of government agencies in order to store information on private citizens. Private organisations, such as credit control companies and employers, also hold personal data on their computers. The ability of the computer to rapidly search and analyse the data, and to link up with other computers via the phone line, means that it is technically possible to retrieve and bring together a mass of data on any citizen.
- Developments in personal movement monitoring, such as car recognition systems, which, if installed on highways, would allow the police to track any vehicle.

These developments mean, on the one hand, that the police and other public bodies are better able to maintain law and order. On the other hand, however, they threaten the privacy of ordinary citizens.

a) The Data Protection Act
To safeguard personal privacy, the EEC has laid down codes of practice for the storage and retrieval of personal data on electronic systems. In the UK, these principles are encoded in the *Data Protection Act 1984*.

The Act covers what it calls *data users* and *data subjects*. Data users are 'organisations or individuals who control the contents and use of a collection of personal data, processed, or intending to be processed, automatically'. A data subject is 'an individual to whom personal data relate'. The Act has two key provisions.

- It requires data users to register, with the Data Registrar, the personal data they hold, and how they use it, obtain it, and disclose it.
- It allows a data subject to find out from the Registrar whether an organisation holds data about him, and to obtain a copy of that data.

Note that the use of home computers to store personal data for domestic or recreational purposes is excluded from the Act – so you can keep an electronic address book on your home computer system. Personal data held in offices on manual systems – such as card index systems – are also excluded.

Besides these two main provisions, the Data Protection Act also requires that personal data must be:

- obtained and processed fairly and lawfully;
- held and used only for the specified purposes;
- adequate, relevant, and not excessive to those purposes;
- accurate and kept up to date;
- deleted when it is no longer needed for the specified purposes;
- stored in a system with security measures taken against unauthorised access, alteration, or destruction of the data.

The purpose of this legislation is stated by the Data Registrar to meet the concern 'arising from the threat which misuse of the power of computing equipment might pose to individuals. This concern derives from the ability of computing systems to store vast amounts of data, to manipulate data at high speed and, with associated communications systems, to give access to data from locations far from the site where the data are stored.' (*Data Protection Act Guideline No 1*.)

b) Data security
The security of data held on computer systems is one of the major concerns of the IT age. There are many reasons why people try to gain unauthorised access to systems:

- to find out information on private individuals;
- to defraud a company by altering its accounts;
- to obtain details of plans or processes for industrial espionage purposes;
- to pit their wits against the system, in the case of 'hackers'.

An electronic system, because it requires minimal human oversight, can be tampered with by a sophisticated hacker with impunity, unless safeguards and 'traps' are built into it. This is especially so today, with the increasing use of telecommunications to access computer systems remotely.

In that the intention of the hobbyist hacker is not normally malicious, he performs the useful function of pinpointing loopholes in security procedures. This is because many hackers tell their victims how they broke through their security.

Other people break into computer systems with a more sinister intent. Computer fraud, which may involve the electronic transfer of company funds to private accounts, has cost some large companies hundreds of thousands of pounds, and has even caused a few small companies to abandon computerised account systems completely and revert to manual systems. The full extent of computer fraud is unknown.

Another problem is the computer programmer with a grudge against the company. He may secretly tamper with the software. Nothing happens while his name remains on the payroll, but if he is dismissed, so that his name is removed, hidden routines are activated, causing the system to behave unpredictably and corrupting data.

It is difficult for an organisation to protect its electronic systems completely against tampering. Often, a system of complex and closely-guarded passwords is used, coupled with a system that allows only certain terminals with special electronic 'signatures' to access confidential data.

There will also normally be several levels of security. At the lowest level is data which is not at all confidential – this can be freely retrieved and read, but the ability to amend it will be restricted to authorised users only. At a higher level is data which is confidential – this can be retrieved and read by authorised users only. The higher the degree of confidentiality, the greater will be the restriction on access.

Assignment 6

Working in a group with one or two others from your class, select one of the topics covered in Chapter 9 and Chapter 10, such as the integrated home or the effect of IT on retailing. Research this topic, then produce suitable audio-visual materials that illustrate and explain the developments that are taking place in it.

These might take the form of a computer 'slide show' produced on a package such as Showpartner on the PC, or Hypercard on the Mac. Alternatively a wall chart or poster might be produced. After being graded by your tutor, the materials produced by the class might form the basis of an IT exhibition.

Questions

1 Why might the introduction of the integrated factory result, initially, in an increase in employment?
2 In a sales office, one clerk handles orders from all customers, another deals with credit control, a third deals with the production of sales documentation, and a further clerk deals

with any queries or complaints that arise from customers re. late orders, damaged goods, etc. How might the work of this office be reorganised so that the clerks have more fulfilling and stimulating jobs?

3 Your tutor intends to computerise the records he keeps of your assignment and exam grades. Advise him on the procedures he should adopt to conform with the requirements of the Data Protection Act.

Answers
to Questions

Answers to Questions

Chapter 1

1 The advantages include: greater speed; higher quality (including greater accuracy); more parts of the job are automated, so reducing the labour requirements; less space required.

2 A computer consists of an input device to capture data, a storage device to store it, a processing device, and an output device to communicate the results of the processing.

3 01000100.

4 8 Kbytes = 1024 × 8 = 8192 bytes. This is 8192 × 8 = 65536 bits. (If we take the approximation that 1 Kbyte = 1000 bytes, then the answer is 64000 bits.)

5 Each byte represents one letter, so one word will require around 6 bytes. One page will therefore require around 2500 bytes, so 8K will store around three pages.

6 One advantage is that many types of IT equipment can be directly connected to the phone network. (At present the digital computer output has to be converted to analogue form using a modem.) A second is that modern digital devices and optic fibres can be incorporated more easily in the network to handle the calls.

Chapter 2

1 The Amstrad PCW is a very cheap system which would meet his needs perfectly adequately. An IBM-PC clone (such as an Amstrad 1640) will cost rather more, but it is a much more capable system which will enable him to cope with a wider range of tasks in the future. For example, he might wish to expand into building extensions, in which case he could make use of some of the sophisticated drawing and design software available on that machine. So the answer depends on Joe's ambitions for the future.

2 a) The development of the silicon chip, resulting in small, low-cost, and powerful microcomputers. b) The rise of the IBM-compatible range of machines, which set a standard for software houses and purchasers. c) Developments in associated hardware, such as laser printers for desktop publishing.

3 Home computers are normally 8-bit machines, which means that for complex business tasks they may be rather slow; and they cannot run complex programs owing to their limited memory. They also generally use cassette tape for storage instead of magnetic disk, which is much too slow and unreliable for business use. Another major drawback is that the software written for these machines generally lacks the features required by business.

4 The mouse enables you to move around the screen very rapidly, and to select and execute options with great ease. It is also much better than the keyboard for producing pictures with drawing and painting software.

5 Laser printers are very fast, they are almost silent in operation, they produce high quality text with a wide range of enhancements, and they are good for graphics. They are ideal for desktop publishing.

Chapter 3

1 Advantages include the fact that moving around the screen and selecting options is very fast, easy, and intuitive, and the use of windows can make your path through a sequence of

tasks very clear. One disadvantage is that you have to move one hand from the keyboard in order to use the mouse; another is the slight additional cost of the extra hardware (i.e. the mouse).

2 One advantage of WIMP software is the fact that it avoids the need to learn operating system commands. Another is that it provides a uniform environment for those software packages that make use of it, so cutting down the learning time. A disadvantage is that it resides in RAM alongside the operating system, and so uses up some of the (limited) memory in PC/ATs.

3 Office work tends to be highly varied, and large, expensive computers can only be effectively used for large jobs. Hence the need for small low-cost computers. Because the world of the office has lagged behind other parts of industry for so long in being automated, it has had a lot of catching up to do.

Chapter 4

1 a) Many legal documents consist of standard paragraphs. These can be stored on disk and inserted as required time and time again in different documents. b) On an estate, most houses have similar characteristics and dimensions. Text describing one house can therefore be used, with minor modifications, for others. c) The body of many of these letters will be the same, only the addresses will differ. With a word processing system the letter need only be written once, and then numerous differently addressed copies produced, either by using mailmerge or else by retyping just the names and addresses.

2 Productivity: mistakes can be corrected on the screen, so eliminating re-typing; text that is common to many documents can be re-used; facilities like search-and-replace can speed up many operations.
Quality: Tippex and overtyping are eliminated by on-screen editing; spelling is improved through the use of electronic spell checkers; if the printed appearance does not look right, it is a quick and easy job to alter the margins etc. and reprint.

3 WP: letters to parents or selected parents, perhaps using mailmerge; internal memos to staff.
DTP: design of forms; school magazines and brochures.

4 Developing the outline of an assignment; maintaining a 'to do' list of tasks to be done; developing and organising revision notes for a subject under appropriate headings and sub-headings.

5 Advantages include: you have complete control over the job; jobs can be done faster, as there are no delays, e.g. in the post or through fitting in with the typesetter's schedules; jobs can be done more cheaply using your own staff; you can quickly and easily make changes to your publication.
Disadvantages are: your own staff using the DTP system may lack design skills; the capital cost of buying the DTP system and training staff to use it; the finished result has not got quite the same high-quality resolution (dots per inch) as the typesetter can achieve.

6 The reason is that the WP package may not be able to support fonts and effects such as kerning, which create excellent looking results.

Chapter 5

1 a) Advantages of using a database package are: he can easily retrieve records of particular students and groups of students, and sort the records into order; he can produce a variety of reports from the data; he can use the database for mailmerge tasks, such as producing end-of-year letters to students.
b) Advantages of using a spreadsheet package are: he can see at a glance a large number of entries; totals and other results are instantly calculated and seen; charts and graphs can be produced to display the main features of the results. c) An integrated package might be best, or possibly a package like Q&A with links to a spreadsheet like Lotus. This software allows you to analyse your data using both approaches.

2 a) Two possible database applications are: customers names and addresses, with the amounts owed and the amounts paid; stock records. b) Two possible spreadsheet applications are: invoicing; to list the time and materials used on a job, with the prices, to calculate the total job cost.

3 +D31+C32.

Chapter 6

1 This baud rate is approximately equal to 2000 characters per second. So 20 000 characters will be sent in ten seconds, which is equivalent to eight pages.

2 Micronet, as part of Prestel, is a menu-driven system and therefore easier to learn and use than CIX. Also, it provides access to other services on Prestel, such as telex. CIX, however, has much more in it that is likely to be of interest, especially for computer users, and provides plenty of opportunities for electronic conversations with other like-minded people.

3 Advantages include: instant delivery, possible lower costs, and access to computer facilities such as multiple mailings of the same message. The disadvantages include the fact that relatively few people can be contacted by this means, and some recipients may not check their mailboxes very frequently.

4 There is a vast amount of information available on-line, far more than in a single library; the information can be accessed at high speed, using the retrieval facilities of the host computer; information in electronic form can be kept up-to-date much more easily than information in a book.

Chapter 7

1 Both the radio and the cassette tape recorder are analogue systems, and therefore cause some degradation of the signal. The cumulative effect could cause a slight loss of data, and make it impossible to load the software into the computer.

2 Data communications between computers.

3 The very high frequency transmissions are of a high quality and unlikely to cause corruption of data, and reflection via satellite is a very reliable system. Ordinary radio broadcasts over a long distance are prone to a great deal of noise, especially when the ionosphere breaks up, and will cause considerable corruption of the computer data.

4 Videophones and videoconferencing.

Chapter 8

1 To produce notices; to produce OHP transparencies for use in lectures; to produce charts and graphs illustrating student statistics.

2 The material is attractively presented and appealing; the learner can be frequently tested and provided with feedback on performance; his route through the material can be adjusted to meet his needs; he is not embarrassed by making wrong answers when a machine is in charge; he can proceed at his own time and pace.

3 It is a digital storage medium; it is robust and unaffected by repeated use; it can store vast amounts of information and is therefore suitable for large databases or multimedia applications.

4 Advantages include: very compact storage medium which is relatively inexpensive to produce; the stored information, being in electronic form, can be easily updated; computer retrieval facilities can be used, e.g. to find all entries on a particular topic.

Chapter 9

1 When applied to production planning, DP enables businesses to plan more accurately and quickly, which means they can hold less in the way of buffer stocks. Lower stock levels mean lower expenditure, and therefore improved cash flows.

2 The use of automatic 'tools' for drawing, scaling, rotating, and so on; the fact that designs of individual components, saved on disk, can be incorporated in many drawings; the fact that designs can be modified with great ease on the screen.

3 Hairdressing requires extremely fine visual and tactile sensing, far superior to what's currently available for robots. Also, few people would want their hair done by robots.

4 The manufacturer can hold lower stocks; the customer can obtain quick delivery of a customized product.

5 Automatic and accurate entry of prices by bar-code readers; automatic updating of stock levels.

6 With the variety of products now available, and the rapid changes in product design, a number of manuals may be required, and these will quickly become out of date. Data in electronic form can be kept up to date and can be quickly accessed. As well as this, the expert system, by the questions it asks, guides the repairman in the tests that he should make to identify faults.

Chapter 10

1 This effect is due to the manpower required to develop the technology and the equipment, and to construct the factories.

2 The sales office currently exemplifies the production-line approach. To make the job more fulfilling, the whole-task approach should be adopted. One way would be to split the customers into four groups – perhaps on the basis of geographical region or type of customer – and give each clerk responsibility for all the work for one of those groups. So an individual clerk would receive and process orders for a group of customers, look after the credit control aspect, and deal with any follow-up queries. That way he or she will deal with all stages of an order.

3 He should ensure that this is covered by any registration that has been made by your college with the Data Registrar; the data should be deleted from the computer system within a reasonable time of your course ending; he must ensure that the data is kept secure, not able to be accessed by unauthorised people.

INDEX

Index

Chambers Commercial Reference Series

COMPUTER TERMS

Sandra Carter

Computer Terms is a compact but comprehensive guide to the key computer words and phrases used in the commercial world.

- Straightforward alphabetical listing

- Helpful jargon-free explanations

- Clear simple layout for easy use

Chambers Commercial Reference Series

Straightforward guides to all the essential terms used in the business world. Ideal for students on a wide range of introductory business and vocational courses. Written in clear, simple English.

Bookkeeping and Accounting Terms
Anthony Nielsen

Business Law Terms
Stephen Foster

Business Terms
John Simpson

Computer Terms
Sandra Carter

Economics Terms
John Samuel Dodds

Marketing Terms
Martin H Manser

Office Practice Terms
Elizabeth King

Printing and Publishing Terms
Martin H Manser

Chambers Commerce Series